*Ending Marriage,
Keeping Faith*

J. Randall Nichols, Ph.D.

Ending Marriage, Keeping Faith

A New Guide Through the Spiritual Journey of Divorce

CROSSROAD · NEW YORK

1993

The Crossroad Publishing Company
370 Lexington Avenue, New York, NY 10017

Printed in the United States of America

Library of Congress Cataloging-in-Publication Data

Nichols, J. Randall.
    Ending marriage, keeping faith : a new guide through the spiritual
journey of divorce / J. Randall Nichols.
        p. cm.
    Includes index.
    ISBN 0-8245-1089-5; 0-8245-1209-X (pbk.)
    1. Divorce—Religious aspects—Christianity.   I. Title.
BT707.N53   1991
248.8'423—dc20   91-2033
                                                      CIP

To Matthew and Adam
who brought to this journey their own brave provisions
of honesty, grace, and humor

AND

To Marcia
who was waiting at the end

Acknowledgments

IT IS IN THE NATURE of things that most of the people who helped me write this book must remain anonymous. They are my psychotherapy clients, members of various groups of divorcing people I have worked with, students, and friends whose struggles and situations form the empirical backdrop of what you will read here. One of the things that humbles me as a therapist is the trust people offer as they give me their various experiences, hopes, and dreams to hold for a short while as we work together.

A friend and teaching colleague, Dr. Freda A. Gardner, once commented to me after returning from an extended tour of churches her former students served as pastors that she was awed by the incredible daily heroism displayed by the people she met as they did nothing more dramatic than live their workaday lives. That is what you will read about in these pages: the incredible daily heroism of men and women trying to keep their footing and their bearings as they journey through the emotional maelstrom of divorce. For their trust and openness I am deeply in debt.

The people I can name in thanks have been generous and supportive at every step of the way, both of my writing and of my own divorce experience. Dr. Elizabeth Johnson of New Brunswick Theological Seminary brought both her incisive biblical scholarship and her pastoral sensitivity to the two chapters about divorce in the Bible. Dr. Robert E. Buxbaum, in my estimation the dean of psychotherapists in the Southwest, has been a constant source of dialogue and suggestion and has provided more than one occasion for me to "field-test" parts of the book with continuing education groups of clergy and therapists. My colleagues on the staff at Trinity Counseling Service have not only encouraged this project but brought their own formidable expertise to bear on its contents, both formally and informally.

Finally, and closest of all to home, Marcia, my wife, has not only supported a sometimes harried author in the concluding stages of this writing as only she in all the world could do but has turned to it both her incredibly penetrating mind and her own rich experience. It was her love and presence that let me type the last lines of this manuscript a very different and vastly more thankful person than the man who began it.

Contents

x   *Contents*

Prologue

EVERYTHING WAS THE SAME—the candles on the table, the Handel from the stereo, the boys, my wife, a Sunday evening meal—and of course nothing was the same. Some inner chime struck, out of key and a little late, but it was time. The dishes were cleared; I looked around the kitchen, listened to my sons now off in their rooms, wondered how it could be ending so quietly, so much as it had begun.

I went to my children separately, noting their dry-eyed

engagement with homework, television, whatever would serve to get them through this moment they had known was coming. To everybody and to nobody I said the only thing I could think to say, the shortest speech of my life, "Well, I'll be going now," and walked out into the evening.

A few moments later the melodrama ended. Halfway down the road I realized I had forgotten something and drove back to retrieve it. What it was I can't recall, but it was in Matthew's room. I found him crying quietly on the bed, sat down and held him for a long time, rocking back and forth like a baby—which of us was which was hard to tell. I left again, holding my wife one last time. "I'm sorry we couldn't make it," I said, or some such useless thing, on the verge of tears, and this time really did it. Was that a comic redemption, I wondered, having to leave twice in one hour? Couldn't you even manage the exit right? Why did you forget that simple thing, whatever it was?

It would take me a year to find out, and a year to cry. But save for the legal timetable that would run its automatic course, my marriage was over. We had ended it the best we could, and I was satisfied we had done it well. Next to raising children, separating was probably the best thing we had ever done together. That wasn't a bitter thought, nor is it now as I write about it. It was just the truth; that is what hurt so much—and still does.

Introduction

AT MY LAST COUNT there were 343 books in print about divorce, and a large number more out of print but still available in libraries. Why in heaven's name add another title to the list? I have two reasons, and understanding them will give you something of the aim and flavor of this book.

In the first place, very few of those books even mention, let alone centrally deal with, something I believe presses on nearly everybody going through it, whether or not they are explicitly religious or churchly, namely what I would broadly speaking call the "spiritual" or "valuational" and even religious dimension of the divorce experience. What a curious gap that is, especially when you consider that most of us got married in a torrent of more or less religious words, which I can testify from my experience as a clergyman even the least sectarian of couples took seriously at the time. It takes far more of a cynic than I am to say that when marriages fail, those words and the feelings, commitments, and beliefs they reflected have lost all their gravitational pull on our humanly wounded minds and hearts. We may not have thought about anything but the mundane hurly-burly of married life for years, but when marriage ends, some level of our consciousness steals its way back to that earlier time and its noble hope and promise, carried on those ceremonial words. Those are the people—far more of us than you would ever count in a church census—and that is the dimension—the more than mundane, spiritual part of the whole business, call it what you will—that this book is about.

It is not just a neglect of the subject that worries me, however, but also what I would have to call a mishandling of it. All too often writings that do enter the spiritual dimension are less than helpful either to the divorcing person or to people like ministers who wish to aid them, either because they seem to have lost human sensitivity in their zeal for piety or because their theological underpinnings are, to put it bluntly, dubious. Again and again through my own separation and divorce I yearned for the kind of written help I seldom found, something that would be emotionally and socially on target but also take seriously the spiritual issues that for me and thousands like me are as important a part of the experience as agreeing on child support or coming to terms with lost dreams. I didn't want to be preached to or lectured or "forgiven" in that sweetly and slyly accusing way so many religious writers have such a nasty habit of doing. I wanted to say to the authorial world, "Look, I am a highly secular, even irreverent man who also walks a spiritual path and takes it seriously. Will anybody talk to me about it?"

Suddenly an image shifted in my thinking. Like most of us in that situation, I believe, I had been thinking of divorce as some kind of falling away—from what people expected, from what I had hoped, from what society approved, from what was accepted as right. I am not much of a hiker, but divorce, as it was mostly being talked about, felt like losing the trail and wandering in the wilderness. I could remember as a child, when divorce was at least a public rarity if not a statistical one, thinking that what it all meant was chaos and confusion, losing the thread, living beyond the pale, dropping out of the race.

Now, though, I had a different thought. Yes, there certainly is a lot of wilderness, pain, and confusion round about people caught in divorce. But was it possible that in my divorce I had not so much fallen off the edge of the spiritual earth as perhaps begun a pilgrimage of a very different kind? *Could divorce, too, be seen as a kind of journey rather than as an absolute ending?* And could we possibly talk about the religious aspects of it—all those broken vows, for instance—in the same way, as some form of spiritual journey? I believe we can talk that way, and that is the guiding image of this book. Divorce is not falling off the path of life, it is taking a different one. That path is, I believe, invariably and inescapably painful at least to some degree, no matter how smoothly or civilly the marital ending goes; but those who walk it are involved in a *process* that has to do with the deepest springs of who they sense themselves to be, what they are now worth, and how they are regarded not only by society but by whatever name they put to that cosmic purpose, destiny, and presence many call God. That process should not only be taken seriously but *talked about,* and in the main it has not been. Whether the pain of divorce is ultimately healing and restoring or simply an excruciating new life partner, bitter exchange for the old one, depends in part, I believe, on whether we who experience it can come to see it as such a journey—with direction, recognizable features, companionship along the way, and finally a safe ending.

Furthermore, I want to talk in ways that have not often been done to people involved in divorce who, in one way or another, concern themselves with what I think we had better start calling its "theological" side. I have searched for just the right term to describe what I mean here without misleading anyone or putting them off, and frankly it has eluded me. "Spiritual" is correct, but it runs the risk of sounding much more otherworldly or pious than I mean. "Religious" would be right in one sense, but certainly not in a sectarian or dogmatic one. "Theological" certainly applies, but I am all too aware that most lay people are as allergic to that term as I am to peanuts—which is "very." My hope is that by doing this initial verbal sputtering I can paint something of a picture of what the book is about. It is about the domain of life that contains our deepest feelings about and commitments to what is most important to us, beyond the everyday boundaries of ordinary human experience.

When I told people about the book as it was being written, they invariably asked me, "But is it *only* for church people?" and often expressed the hope that it would not be. It is not. Yes, I have chosen to write out of the theological context I know best, which is the Christian church, but I am certainly talking also to people who would not identify themselves as either very actively or even passively religious, whether Jewish or Christian. Divorce has a way of bringing some people into the church or temple and driving others away; but for almost everyone it raises

questions about ultimate meanings and concerns, regardless of the religious or theological language one speaks.

The second reason I am writing this book is simpler and
more personal. Even though I am going to be talking
about feelings, ideas, and perspectives that are not clearly
autobiographical, this is really my own story, and over the
years I have come to cherish such writing from others.
Again and again I find myself turning to the personal history, the intimate recollection, the autobiography, the
memoir as the most accessible way into the most important subjects. That may be far too heady a buildup to this
modest book, but I simply wanted to tell you why I did it
this way, perhaps as a way of reaching some agreement
between us, author and reader, about what to expect. It is,
I suppose, a combination of memoir and commentary. It is
not purely a journal, though I not only try to use my own
experience but also include flashbacks of writing done as I
went through it all. It is not purely a theoretical piece,
though as you will see I have ideas about the spiritual and
theological ways we have understood divorce that are
sometimes sharply different from the usual, and I do try to
make a case for them.

In this connection it seems appropriate to say a quick
word about who I am and what business, if any, I have
writing this book. I am a Presbyterian minister who both
teaches in a theological seminary and practices individual
and marital psychotherapy in a large counseling service.
Both as a therapist and formerly as a parish pastor I have
worked a lot with people going through divorce, and
though none of us ever ceases to marvel at the richness
and diversity of the human experiences that come our
way, I nevertheless suppose I have been involved with as
full a spectrum as anyone of marriages and divorces, from
best to worst, civilized to barbaric, healthy to sick. Several
years ago my own long-standing marriage reached a point
where its long deferred problems could no longer be ig-

nored, and my wife and I divorced. We had been married for seventeen years, had two boys ages ten and thirteen at the time, and looked to most people like an ideal couple. Because of our commitment to as much personal and emotional honesty as we could muster, we aimed for the "best" divorce we could get, painfully ironic though that sounds, and in many ways I think we did it. Of all the divorce situations I have been involved in professionally, I would have to rank my own among the least destructive, and I thank God for it for our sakes, our children's, our families', and our friends'. *But let me be as clearly emphatic as I can to say that that does not come close to eliminating the hurt and confusion and soul-searching that I believe inevitably and inescapably goes with divorce, no matter how cleanly it is accomplished.* What we gained, and what I hope for you to gain partly as a result of this book, was not an exemption from pain but a chance to emerge more freely on the other side of it than we otherwise might have, than so many others I have seen in fact have.

This book is one of the fruits of that incredibly painful but equally re-creative experience. It is, simply, the kind of book I badly wanted and needed to have myself at the time but could not find. Divorce may be the occasion for the most intense self-examination most of us ever do. I looked in my own mirror and saw first and foremost a confused, hurting human being. But I also had no choice but to see a theologian and a therapist who knew and had experienced more about divorce than most people. Sometimes I cursed that knowledge because it tied me in too many knots of understanding the dynamics of what was happening without freeing me to express and march through the experience. But at other times those roles looking back at me in the mirror got together and said, "You are having to chisel out some new comprehension of yourself and you are having to discard a lot of muddled thinking about divorce, especially from the religious quarter, and, damnit, there are lots of other people out there who need some help doing the same thing." The book began then.

This is not by any means a "complete" book about divorce, as you will already have gathered. The things I am talking about are, by design, things I believe have been either neglected or mishandled in the ways we usually talk. There are many excellent writings about divorce, and I will be mentioning several of them as we go along. Hopefully you either have or will make their acquaintance. I am making no attempt to duplicate or even improve on most of them. It is the idea of divorce as a potentially re-creative journey of the spirit, broadly understood, that concerns me, because that is where time after time we seem to draw a blank.

One of the things I have learned about divorce both in my counseling practice and in my own experience is that virtually anything you say about any aspect of it is going to be wrong for someone. Dogmatic statements are always to be mistrusted (perhaps even that one!) but nowhere more so than in such a complicated and emotionally charged subject as separation and divorce. At the same time, however, there clearly are some things we who go through the experience have in common, and hence there are some things that can be said as guidelines for helping. An image that comes to mind has to do with airplane landings. From where I sat writing most of this book I had a grandstand view of the approach path of a small but busy private airport. One day it occurred to me that I had involuntarily logged a lot of hours myself just watching landings, and I had become something of a sidelines expert. Someone once told me that an airplane landing was no more than a controlled crash, which did not do much for my equanimity in the air but nevertheless offered a useful insight into the process. The crash is inevitable; the question is how well controlled it will be. After months of watching those airplanes make their approaches to land I discovered that I could sort out several different pilot styles and competencies. Some were smooth and relaxed, obviously the work of experienced pilots with good equipment, while others were jerky and a little frantic, coming a little too high or fast. They all "crashed" safely—but the differences in the various landings—and what they must have been like to the people on board—was pretty wide.

You can think of divorces like that. Only rarely, thank God, do things get so out of control that people get killed. Meanwhile some are smooth, others rough; some well planned and executed, others hasty and brittle; some leave passengers shaken to their toes and vowing never to fly again, while others make people grateful for the execution and eager for more. What we are going to do now is try for the best landing we can get, for you if you are going through separation and divorce, or for your divorcing friends or people who come to you for help if that is your situation. I do not know if this book will make it any easier for you; but if it allows you to walk through your own journey a little more freely, lift your eyes a fraction higher toward the horizon, and own a bit more completely your worthwhileness as a potentially loved and loving human being, it will have done what I wanted and hoped.

Ending Marriage,
Keeping Faith

ONE

Divorced Is Not Something You Get

LIKE IT OR NOT, people in divorce are embarked on a journey—whose course and destination are fairly well-known and widely talked about, despite the feelings of uncertainty and disorientation that seem to be well-nigh universal among divorcing people. The place to begin thinking about the aspects of the journey to which this book is devoted is right here, with our basic image of what is involved in "getting divorced." For years I accepted the almost universal notion that the aim of the separation and divorce process was to reach, across a huge and fiery lake of pain, the state of being divorced—emotionally, socially, and relationally as well as legally. As a therapist I had seen all too often what happened when people did not make it across that lake, but instead stayed in some troublesome emotional ways "married," no matter what the courts said. A colleague and I once led a therapy group for divorced women, whose divorces ranged in duration from six months to fifteen years. We wondered at first whether they would be in such different places as to have little in common, but discovered to our surprise—and even greater worry—that none of the women in the group could be said actually to be completely "divorced" in a psychological sense. Some were still grieving their lost marriages in camouflaged ways, others were mired in bitterness and sadness, and virtually none had made much progress, no matter how many years later, in reestablishing social contact with other men. What worried my colleague and I was that, as we put it to ourselves, divorce in the psychological sense had not fully happened for these women. (The significance of another fact about the group would not hit me until years later: they were all active church members, and indeed the therapy was taking place under the auspices of a particular congregation of which I was then the pastor. It never occurred to us then to wonder whether there might be a connection, perhaps something by way of a covert religious message that was *keeping* them incompletely divorced. In the next chapter the meaning of that will come clear!)

My therapist colleagues and I have found much the same thing in our counseling practices. Again and again people come for help on some personal issue that has arisen long after a divorce and apparently is unrelated to it, only to discover in due time that what they are really working on, still, was the seemingly endless trek toward "getting divorced."

The dynamics of delayed grieving seem to be at work. A basic psychological fact of life, now known to most people, is that grieving after a significant loss is a natural healing process that is necessary for recovery. If something happens to block it off, the sense of attachment to what was lost remains in force, preventing people from moving ahead with their lives and *reattaching* their energies elsewhere. Divorce is nothing if not a loss experience of enormously complex dimensions: the loss of a spouse, of dreams and hopes, often of a home, of children, sometimes the loss of a sense of moral worth, the loss quite literally of friends and connections, and on and on. Here was a woman, for instance, divorced for over ten years, who was trying to recover from the loss of a second major love after ending her marriage—or so it seemed. It soon became apparent that what she was really working on unconsciously was the long dead relationship with her ex-husband. Her case was so common, in one variation or another, that over the years I began automatically to assume with my divorced clients that they probably had not "gotten there" until I satisfied myself otherwise. If the goal was to get a divorce over and done with and get on with one's life, as we all assumed, then something was seriously out of kilter somewhere along the line with a large number of people.

My own personal experience had not been much different. When several years after my marriage ended by mutual agreement, I still found myself dreaming about my former spouse, I began to kick myself around the emotional block in anger and embarrassment at not having done a better job of it. The jolt was that I thought I had done the grieving, made the separation, crossed the lake, and just when I would get most secure in that knowledge, something would happen to snap me back to the other side as though I had not done any grief work at all.

A NEW IMAGE FOR THE PROCESS

One day quite by chance, however, I overheard a remark that suddenly opened up a completely different slant on the problem and led me to wonder whether we had formulated the getting-divorced goal wrongheadedly in the first place. The comment was an idea put rather jarringly by a person who said, "We never do get divorced. We are always divorcing." That, of course, went against the grain of everything I had been trained to believe about separation and loss and the emotional process of recovery. Surely we were not being asked just to throw in the towel on our futures and settle for staying stuck in non-marriages that could not quite become divorces! A gloomier prospect I could hardly imagine.

The idea being expressed here, though, was something a bit different. It held that just as marriages do not suddenly come into being with the pronouncement of a few special words but rather have to be built and worked on throughout their lifetimes, so too divorces do not reach a final state of having "happened" but rather *in some sense* have to be worked on long after the legal rituals are concluded—quite possibly for the rest of one's life.

Now here was a subtle distinction of major importance: "getting divorced" was not the objective so much as "divorcing successfully." Just as we would not for a minute think of declaring a marriage a successful accomplishment just because the wedding went beautifully, no more would we declare a divorce to be "accomplished" just because the decree had been issued—that much was obvious. But—to continue the analogy—just when would we say that a marriage had become "complete"? Well, when you stop to think about it, *we wouldn't*. What we would say, perhaps, is that when things went well a couple got to the point that the rhythms of their marriage went along smoothly, accommodating to the ups and downs of life with good communication and relational skills, a certain mutuality and flexibility, and on through a long checklist of things most of us would recognize as the hallmarks not of a marriage that had been "done" but rather of one that was working well.

I now found myself thinking about divorce in the same way. The people who seemed to make it well had not so much achieved a divorced state in which the issues were all over and done with, as they had managed to wage the process of divorce successfully as a long-term operation. *Divorce, like marriage, could be seen as a long-term, even lifetime, process that one managed either well or poorly, as the case might be.* If it was managed well, then certain landmarks would be recognizable, the very things we were accustomed to thinking of as signaling that an emotional divorce had been "gotten." The divorced couple would be unentangled emotionally; anger and bitterness would be to some degree resolved; necessary interactions between former spouses over children, property, and the like would not catapult them back into former destructive behavior patterns; and the spouses would be free to enter into other positive relationships, including, perhaps, remarriage. In other words, the signs of a "successful" divorce were pretty much the same as ever; what had begun to change in my thinking was the basic image of the whole process. What that said more concretely was that a lot of people out there were trying to reach a relational *state* rather than learning how to undertake a relational *process*, and it was no wonder they were having such trouble. The image of finally crossing that fiery lake was wrong from the start; in other words: it is not a matter of reaching the other side and climbing safely onto dry land with no need ever to take that awful trip again. It is more a question of learning how to navigate a complex river system so you are not stuck in a tributary you do not want, even though you are still traveling in what is geographically the same river.

Perhaps we should have tumbled to this even earlier from thinking about the grief aspects of divorce. Studies of the dynamics of grief, most classically following the death of a loved one, are relatively new in psychology, say in the last forty years, and our understanding of grief has grown and changed accordingly in a fairly short period of time. One of the most significant recent changes of thinking has to do with what we take as the successful outcome of normal, healthy grieving. The primary thing we look for is a person's ability to "take back," so to speak, the psychic energy that had been invested in the lost person or object and to reinvest that energy in an appropriate new way. So, for instance, a person experiencing acute grief will typically feel unable to do much of anything for a while; there will be no energy for housework or career or socializing. Slowly but surely, as the grief work proceeds, some of that energy returns. Gradually the grieving person is able to feel toward another person the way he or she did toward the person lost. For a widow of two weeks to think about remarrying is virtually impossible in most cases, because the energy is still attached to the lost spouse. A few years later, if grieving has gone well, things will be very different and reattachment becomes a possibility. We were accustomed, then, to say that the grief work had been "done" and that the grieving was "over," the emotional status quo before the loss having been regained.

Within probably the last dozen years, however, we have changed our minds a lot about that, and the change has to do not so much with the behavior we hope to see as with the underlying idea of what has happened when that positive behavior appears. Most of us who work regularly with such things would now acknowledge that at some level one never "gets over" a significant loss, particularly of an important person, for the simple reason that in such a loss one's history has been permanently changed. Expecting things in time to rebound to the same shape they were before is absurd: *they just are not the same and never will be,* though that does not mean we do not recover from loss, do our grieving, and get on successfully with our lives. The point is that in one way or another coping with that loss is a process, a task that with greater or lesser self-consciousness will always be with us, even though we eventually reach the point that the lost person or object is seldom an active factor in our emotional lives. There is nothing unhealthy or "stuck" about that in and of itself; it is just the way the human experience works. So now the working objective in helping people with major loss is not to get them to go through a certain number of "stages of grief" or any such thing and then pronounce them through with the painful business, so much as it is to help them wage a process that will not always be as intense or conflicted or painful as it may now be, and that may very well recede almost into invisibility as the years go by, but that in some sense will always be a part of their lifework as a human being whose history has been written thus. That is a very different thing from a blocked, stalled, denied, or otherwise uncompleted experience.

Separation and divorce are obviously loss experiences, and clearly grief is a central part of what it means to go through it. We will be talking more about that in chapter nine. The point here is that the same discovery we made about grieving now needs to be made about divorcing. *Divorced is not something you "get"; divorcing is something you do.*

I believe that should be taken as a basic assumption by all divorcing people, but especially by those who are involved with children. Unless one ex-spouse is out of the parenting picture entirely, by choice or design, the former partners are necessarily going to have to have something to do with each other. That is, some sort of working relationship is going to exist even though it is not a married one. What is the relationship then? Well, it is a divorcing one, and it has its own peculiar dynamics. It is a journey to be taken rather than a destination to be reached. For instance, when an ex-spouse, even years later, discovers that he or she is still emotionally involved with a former mate, perhaps the response should not be to worry that one hasn't "made it" yet through divorce but rather to ask whether the divorcing experience is going along as, by whatever lights we have, it should.

Please do not misunderstand me to be saying that if you are divorcing you are forever going to be in the same soup you may feel yourself in right now. Looking ahead for myself, for instance, I hope and anticipate there will come a time when the flashes of regret or anger or loneliness I still have will be so rare I scarcely notice them. Let me offer a personal for-instance. During the time I was divorced I could see with real relief that my former marriage was less and less an unwanted "chaperon" in my new relationships with women friends. At first it was like always dating two women, which made for some emotionally very expensive social life even if the credit card slips did not show it. Now that is not so, and I expect things to continue to get better, especially with a new wife. What I do not expect, however, nor would I ever want to, is no longer to be conscious of myself as a person who spent a long time in a marriage that finally ended. I will not be dwelling on the former marriage, but if I am responsible I will be aware of my own self and history. That is the point. Nor does this new image of the divorce process need to leave us without some bench marks to measure our progress. That is the subject to which we now turn.

YOUR FIRST FIVE DIVORCES[1]

Several books about divorce speak helpfully of various stages or phases of the experience, on the analogy of stages of grief work in death situations. As long as we are careful to remind ourselves that such stages have a habit of occurring out of order and doubling back on themselves, I find those schemes useful in sorting out what can be a massive overflow of stimulation and information when marriage ends.

What they do, to borrow a term familiar in family therapy circles, is provide a way of "punctuating" our experience. Punctuation, as we all drearily remember from English grammar classes, is a system using such otherwise meaningless symbols as periods and commas whereby a string of words is divided up to make more sense than it would if we just let it all run together. The very word means to "point," and that is the underlying idea: to point to places in a sentence where meaning changes, as for instance when reaching the end of a thought, or encountering an idea that poses a question. Everyday experience itself is "punctuated" in a metaphorical way by ideas we use to divide it up into manageable and meaningful chunks. When a person we live with scowls and growls at something we have done, for instance, we may think to ourselves that the reason for such behavior is that he or she is angry with us, and that very idea is a way of "punctuating" the immediate experience, or linking it up to other immediate experience in such a way that it has

[1] After writing this section I came across a helpful book by Harold Straughn entitled *The Five Divorces of a Healthy Marriage: Experiencing the Stages of Love* (St. Louis: CPB Press, 1986). It is a useful book, also in the vein of offering a way of "punctuating" a larger overall experience, but not at all the same thing that we are talking about here. The similar images were arrived at independently.

meaning for us. Another way of punctuating it might be to think that the dyspeptic behavior comes not from anger at us but rather from a bad day at the office or physical discomfort or too much to drink, or whatever other idea may occur to us as a way of making sense of what we are experiencing—punctuating it.

The idea of *divorcing* rather than *getting divorced* as the image of our objective is a way of punctuating the whole experience, relating its various parts to each other so that we can make sense of it all. As a form of punctuation I have come to think not so much of stages of divorce as of successive "divorces," each with its own peculiarities and major events. Even if it is no more than a different metaphor, counseling clients with whom I use this scheme seem to find it helpful, once they are over the initial shock of envisioning themselves divorced five times from one marriage! Each "divorce" has a characteristic positive outcome which, when reached, helps us move along in the process so that we are more successfully divorcing as we go.

THE FIRST DIVORCE

What I will call the "first divorce" for a couple typically occurs long before anyone talks (or perhaps even thinks) overtly about ending the marriage. *This is the experience, which at first can be quite unconscious, of one or both partners' losing the motivation and energy needed to sustain a marriage.* Life may go along pretty much as usual, such is the binding power of routine and habit, but the relational "glue" just loses its strength, probably over a period of a fairly long time and for lots of different reasons. Like an old chair in which the same thing has happened, it still may see a lot of use before some unaccustomed stress makes it collapse under a startled occupant.

A lot of couples come for marriage counseling because this first divorce either has already happened or a couple is afraid it is about to. In fact, I would tend to divide the couples I have worked with into two broad categories. One includes couples whose basic relationship, I soon come to see, has a lot of motive power and solidity to it but who are experiencing one or more troublesome issues they want (and need) to work on. The presenting picture can be pretty horrendous, even still, and counseling may take a very long time even with the relational glue basically sound and resilient. This is not necessarily a category of "easy" counseling, and couples may be at very high risk if something is not done to help them; but one just gets a sense in working with such people that unless something happens to make things a lot worse, the existence of the marriage itself is not an issue. "First divorce" has not occurred, unlike with the couples in the second category for whom it clearly has, whether they know it or not. It is with this second group, I believe, that what the public tends to identify as "failures" in marriage counseling most often occur (though as you will see later in Chapter Twelve, I want to argue pretty strongly that "failure" is often misunderstood). Indeed, a fair number of couples who have experienced "first divorce" seem almost instinctively to seek out something that will give them "permission" to acknowledge it and move toward ending the marriage, even if the process is quite unconscious. Perhaps it will be an extramarital relationship, or a spouse's response to an external source of stress, or even what happens in counseling itself that finally tips the chair. The point is that the glue was already gone.

Here may be a good place for a brief aside about a phenomenon some researchers believe is increasing, the failure of long-term marriages. We are awash in printed material about mid-life crises, especially for males, and how they impact marriages. I have no doubt about the importance of the dynamics of mid-life transitions, but I find myself rather skeptical that they cause divorces. I myself have never, in quite a few years as a marital therapist, encountered a "mid-life marriage failure" such as the popular magazines seem to be full of, where one spouse (typically the husband) reacts to his mid-life experience by flinging away from a marriage that was otherwise in good shape. What I have found, however, is that a lot of marriages *in which "first divorce" has already occurred* unconsciously and perhaps with great relief "use" the mid-life experience as a way of getting permission to move on with the already started divorcing process. If that is happening more these days, perhaps it is because some social and economic and even religious constraints on divorce are a bit more relaxed. That is not at all the same thing, however, as saying that some mysterious, virus-like component of mid-life experience puts marriages in jeopardy. Changing senses of self, vocation, and fulfillment at mid-life, as well as changed situations in family economics, child-rearing, physical attributes, and the like all impact marriages and often exact their prices in needs for adjustment and work. I know of no evidence, however, that links any of these things to marital failure if the basic motivation and commitment of the partners to their marriage is intact. (It certainly is true, by the same token, that there are lots of marriages out there in which "first divorce" has long since occurred that are going to endure, with greater or lesser happiness, to the end. As you will see in later pages, I am frankly skeptical of automatically putting a spiritual seal of approval on such arrangements.)

There is a strong positive value in recognizing one's first divorce, whether it leads to the end of a marriage or not, and that is the clarification of the corrosive confusion that most times has settled in on such a marriage. Sometimes the crystallization of conflict, so that at long last we know what it is we are dealing with, brings great release to the people involved. It is not that there is no pain, but rather that the even worse experience of not having any idea what is wrong goes away. I have seen couples who were devoting almost unbelievable amounts of energy to trying to hold their relationship together after first divorce had occurred become worlds more free and energized when the old chair finally collapsed and they knew what they had to deal with—whether with divorce or reconstitution of the marriage.

THE SECOND DIVORCE

When living together becomes intolerable because of the first divorce, the second one takes place: here is the actual separation of two marriage partners, with all the difficult dynamics and actual arrangements that are so often talked about. The most significant thing I want to say about it is that even though coming to a decision to separate may have taken enormous time and energy to reach, it is still a very early part of the divorcing process. Second divorce is sometimes the first public sign that a marriage is ending, but it by no means accomplishes the work even when the couple themselves have no doubts about wanting the marriage to end.

An editorial by Edna O'Brian describes second divorce poignantly and a little humorously when she writes, "We do not quite utterly want to leave, we want to leave for the most part, but there is one small tug that keeps us behind. It is not love, it is not even decency, it is either terror or that nice dull daily balm known as habit."[2] She goes on to describe how this "one small tug" so often takes the form of some insignificant personal effect left behind, perhaps "accidentally." "Whether it's a garment or a pearl necklace it does not matter, it is merely proof of indecision and

[2] Edna O'Brian, "Hers," editorial, *The New York Times*, Sept. 12, 1985, p. C-2.

fuels the thoughts that yield up a bounty of mad hope and a bed of wretchedness."[3] When I read the piece, months after my "second divorce," I ruefully remembered that now forgotten object that took me home again minutes after leaving, mute, unconscious testimony to this part of the process.

Because the grief of separation can be acute, it is both terribly difficult and terribly important to make second divorce as complete and intentional as possible, but with as many elements of previous support systems intact as possible. That may not be an easy combination to manage, but trying to do so matters a lot for the parts of the journey yet to come. I worry about two extremes. On one extreme, households may completely dissolve with both spouses and children relocating, necessitating new schools, friends, jobs, community services, and all the rest. And on the other, spouses may do the minimum readjusting necessary, almost as though to pretend it had not happened. The departing spouse takes a sparsely furnished room rather than an apartment, and subtly continues to live out of his or her former house, even if only in fantasy.

The positive outcome of second divorce is the recovery of a great deal of energy, which in time will be used to reinvest in other commitments, other work, and other people. Especially when a lengthy planning or decision-making process has gone before, a person in second divorce may discover reserves of energy unsuspected for years. It may, in fact, be a blow to realize that yet another divorce lies just around the corner.

[3] *Ibid.*

THE THIRD DIVORCE

Let us assume for just a moment, as actually happened in my own case, that the second divorce has gone well, with a clean break, good lines of necessary communication with the separated spouse, the children responding appropriately, and so on. I had moved to an apartment two miles down the same road from where I had lived, and because by nature I am a homebody and a "nester," I had gotten the apartment furnished and operating quickly and well. It was to be a transitional arrangement for a year or two while we worked out the "divorce" itself and decided what could be done about a house for me in due time. The flow of energy was high, partly because I had mortgaged so much of it during the previous few years working on and worrying about my marriage and now was able to reclaim it, and partly because new adventures into cooking, building new friendships, and managing my own turf pulled it out of me. Yes, there was pain and loneliness and all the rest; but things were "going well," just as I had hoped and planned they would.

But then a year later suddenly things were not going so well, and though I did not know how to put it at the time, *I ran rather solidly and painfully into what I now call "third divorce." That is the time when you realize, in retrospect, that in some ways all this time you have been only role-playing a divorcing person, and now the reality hits full force.* Then is the time for the third divorce. In all my careful preparations for single living I had necessarily left some things behind in the large house my wife and I lived in for nearly ten years. We had agreed in writing that certain items would be mine but would remain behind until I occupied a house where they could be accommodated. Those seemingly purely physical artifacts proved to carry a great deal more emotional meaning than I would ever have suspected. There were a lot of large aquariums, since at one time tropical fish had been a consuming passion—consuming both me and an unconscionable amount of floor space. There was a nine-foot grand piano that had been especially important to me, partly because of interest in music, partly because of strong childhood associations, and partly in hope my children would learn to play (they didn't). There were boxes of books, lovingly collected antique encyclopedias among them, and a variety of other things in the hobbies-and-interests department that had always meant a great deal to me.

Just in case it needed proving yet another time that a person whose business is being attuned to subtle feelings and meanings is sometimes oblivious to his or her own, I simply failed to realize that these things I had left behind, which carried such large personal significance for me, also blunted for me the reality of the separation. So long as these things of mine were "at home," some major part of me had not left. Until I collected all my things—and all myself—I was only playing a role at divorcing. When I finally did move those things into an already cramped apartment, the space was jammed but I was not. My third divorce had happened, bringing with it that special kind of freedom that only comes when facades collapse and one lives more fully into the reality of his or her situation, no matter how difficult it may be.

I can write a little lightheartedly about it now; it assuredly did not feel that way at the time. I see now that it was even more confusing for my wife, because the parts of ourselves that we leave behind, symbolically, convey a mixed message: is he or she coming back or not? Here is the positive value of third divorce: it can straighten out the mixed emotional messages separated spouses send each other and end their misleading destructiveness. I had certainly not consciously intended all that stuff of mine to suggest either to me or to my wife that perhaps all this upheaval was not real after all and would not last; but that was what it did, willy-nilly, until the third divorce occurred.

THE FOURTH DIVORCE

As I write, it strikes me that first divorce had a kind of fatigued quality to it, second divorce seemed energized, and third divorce was almost faintly comic. Fourth divorce, however, to me and to those of you who have shared your journeys with me, is pain. *Here is the time in our divorcing when either in reality or in fantasy we try to go back to the marriage, and discover that it does not work.*

Third and fourth divorces sometimes blur together, particularly if a person approaching third divorce tries to head it off by going back to the marriage. I prefer to treat them as separate events, however, just because the feelings and inner dynamics seem very different, no matter that calendar-wise they may be hard to distinguish.

Any number of things can trigger the urge to go back and try it again, either in fantasy or in reality, though it would probably be more accurate to say that going back is a natural inclination that comes with the territory and merely needs a little push to surface. Three that seem to be most common are children, loneliness, and failed new relationships, though of course the list is probably almost as long as there are individual divorces. When young children are involved, the universal assumption is that divorce is a wrenching experience that is hard for them, and responsible parents will quite naturally want to alleviate as much of that pain as possible. Again and again I hear separated parents wonder aloud whether for the sake of the kids they shouldn't try it again, thinking that surely it would not be as bad this time. The kids, meanwhile, will almost certainly pick up this vacillation at least in unconscious ways and proceed to make it worse by letting you know just how awful their experience is. It is nearly miraculous how when a parent gets through fourth divorce and loses most of his or her ambivalence about it, the children suddenly seem to be having a better time of it, with few complaints and dislocations. My own children gave me a blunt and rather comic demonstration of the need for divorcing parents to get clear about *whose* pain they are registering at a given moment. Things seemed to be going well with us, so much so that I began to worry that I was overlooking some deep trouble in them. I myself had not felt better in years, and had not yet learned to credit that in itself with having a profound positive impact on the children. One evening we were all sprawled around the living room reading when I decided to be "responsible" and said, "Well guys, we haven't talked for a while about how you're feeling about the separation, and I just want to see how that is for you." A few moments of silence passed while they read on, until one of them looked up and with a touching combination of filial concern and mild disgust replied, "You know, Dad, you're a lot more worried about all this than we are," and then went back to his newspaper.

Loneliness is one of those experiences I would come close to calling universal in divorce, and it does not seem to matter how many people surround you, how glad you were to exit a troubled relationship, or how easy a time of it you are having in separation. Especially with long marriages I think we underestimate the extent to which we come to depend on the established presence of a spouse, negative or positive. I have seen people yearn to go back to a husband or wife whom they freely acknowledge was vicious, unfaithful, self-centered, and hateful—because they are lonely. And if you were the one who did not want the separation, of course, things can be even worse. Yes, being surrounded by friends and even new loves may help, but it does not eradicate the feeling.

Perhaps the most important thing we can do about it is to stop fighting and go "with" the feeling for a time, asking ourselves in fantasy what it would really be like to go back, or looking carefully at the dealings we have with our estranged spouses to see if anything *really* has changed. It is far more useful to do that than to get tied up in knots for fear the loneliness "proves" we made the wrong decision to begin with. Understanding that being lonely is natural, no matter how necessary, right, or welcome the decision to separate was, can help us gain perspective. What we are experiencing is not a "relapse" or a sign of a wrong decision; we are going through the fourth divorce.

I will be talking in Chapter Eleven about some special and often unrecognized dynamics of opposite-sex relationships after separation. The failure of a new relationship, however, can be a powerful impetus to going back and may, in its way, become the midwife of fourth divorce. I remember crying in my separated wife's arms in guilt, fear, and sadness because a woman I thought I had fallen in love with had ended the relationship, and to my surprise and horror I turned back to a woman I no longer loved or wanted to live with for temporary solace—and perhaps benediction. It was not an experience I ever want to repeat, such a mixture was it of grief both for the marriage and for the new relationship, but it got me through fourth divorce. That is the positive outcome of this part of the journey: you move ahead through your grieving, perhaps aided by what I will be calling a "transitional relationship," and are prepared for the fifth divorce, which when successfully done sets us free for the rest of the divorcing journey.

THE FIFTH DIVORCE

The fifth divorce is not especially marked by any of the signal events the others were. *It is the experience of becoming single again internally and emotionally*, and because it has so few external markings, I tend to believe it is one of the hardest divorces to work through. Mind you, I am not referring now to being married or single as a legal or social arrangement, but as an interior matter of self-identification. Here is where we leave behind not a particular spouse or history but the very self-definition of "married person." In first divorce we left the inner motivation for marriage to the particular person we had wed. In second divorce we left the marital home. In third divorce we left the artificial role of ex-spouse. In fourth divorce we left the attempt to go back. Now in fifth divorce we leave being married, period.

It can be a terribly difficult divorce, more so I sometimes think than any of its predecessors. Perhaps that is only to be expected since, after all, most of us had to take a long time to learn how to stop being a single person and become a married one. It required all sorts of often unrecognized shifts in who we saw ourselves to be, how we related to other people, what we valued, and how we sought to actualize it. It should not surprise us that reversing the process takes an equal and opposite amount of time and effort.

I learned about fifth divorce the hard way, from a single, never-married woman I had been seeing and wanted to become more involved with. It was a difficult, on-again, off-again relationship that had probably the highest peaks of pleasure and the deepest pits of despair of any I have ever experienced, for lots of complicated reasons. At one point my friend said to me ("yelled" might be more apt, as

I recall), "The trouble is that you're married inside." Naturally I denied it vigorously, but of course she was right, as I later discovered when I woke up to a shift in me I had not even been aware of. One day with no great fanfare, I looked at myself, the people I was dating, my life-style, my children, my former wife, and said to myself, "I'm not married anymore. I might be again someday and I might like that, but right now I am single and it is the way I want to be." For me the great tip-off was simply that I stopped looking at my female relationships—real or wished-for—as potential marriages. For someone else the reorientation will be signaled differently.

The positive achievement of fifth divorce is that one is free to recommit oneself to another relationship, permanent or not, if one wants to. Here is the elusive goal we were after all along when speaking about "getting divorced." The divorcing journey continues, but when we go through fifth divorce we are very different people than when we started. We are out of the turbulent tributary of our marriage, and though still on the same river we are now in different waters. My friend who startled me so knew this instinctively, that until I became single again I would not be as fully available to her as would have to be the case for our new relationship to have its own identity, let alone future.

This is what worries me about people in divorce who either before or immediately after "second divorce" are intimately involved with another person. Until fifth divorce is reached I believe those relationships are largely transitional, with their own special value perhaps. But if they are to become permanent they must change their character fundamentally somewhere along the line, which is not impossible but is all too often unrecognized. When such couples themselves want to be married and come for counseling, which is usually a very good idea by the way, I now routinely tell them at the beginning that in order to work as a marriage their relationship first has to end. That is, they both have to become single first and then reconstruct their relationship if they are to avoid the pitfall of repeating their earlier marriage(s) with no more than the actors playing the show changing.

Yes, that is an oversimplification, but the underlying dynamic is very powerful and needs, I believe, to be put this bluntly. Fifth divorce is a major milestone with its gift of freedom, but it is fairly far down the line in the divorcing process, which is notorious for exacting payment on all who try to shortcut it. Priceless freedom—not just from a bad marriage but from the corrosive forces which made it that way—is hard to come by. If it were not, you would probably not be reading this or any book, or needing to. That freedom has a lot of enemies along the way, some of them very amiable and well-intentioned and not at all villainous-appearing. To one of the most important of them, particularly for people who take the spiritual perspective seriously, we now must turn.

TWO

The Friendly Divorce Myth

ONE OF THE MOST USEFUL BOOKS about divorce, Bernard Steinzor's *When Parents Divorce: A New Approach to New Relationships,* is now unhappily out of print.[1] It was a heretical book at the time it was published and still is, because in it Steinzor argued persuasively and successfully against one of the most enduring bad ideas of marital separation: the myth of the "friendly divorce." Instead he was

[1] Bernard Steinzor, *When Parents Divorce: A New Approach to New Relationships* (New York: Pantheon Books, 1969).

articulating a very different objective, what he called "divorce with freedom." While I will not make any effort to summarize Steinzor's whole book, I do want to be sure his basic idea stays in circulation, because I believe it is one of the most helpful insights available to the divorcing person on both psychological and spiritual or theological grounds.

The friendly divorce myth takes many forms. Perhaps its purest expression would run something like this. "We are ending a marriage that was plagued by unhappiness and even destructiveness of one kind or another, and in various ways we feel badly about that—about the hurt we have caused and suffered, about the conflicts the children have endured, about the feelings and behavior we had that are so uncharacteristic of us in our better moments, about the lost ideal of our marriage. The least we can do now is be friendly towards each other, certainly for the sake of the children, laying aside the old issues and feelings that need no longer plague us since we are no longer married."

There are many variations on that theme. At one extreme is the person whose anger at the former spouse is unabated and who would just as happily push his or her ex-mate over the nearest cliff if it could be done without repercussion, but who nevertheless promises to go out of his or her way to speak well of and be friendly to the other, especially for the sake of the children. Way over at the other extreme is the former spouse who while acknowledging that the marriage is well and truly over still wants to be "best friends" with the departed wife or husband. In between are any number of other positions, all sharing the basic idea and value that one degree or another of friendship between the ex-spouses is the right and good thing to aim for.

Few of these people are cynics or hypocrites. Most of them in my experience genuinely try to reach their goal, often with agonizing dedication even when their deepest

feelings are straining to go in exactly the opposite direction. They are simply responding to a social and religious
value so deeply rooted, at least in American culture, that
even wondering out loud about it, as Steinzor did and I am
doing, runs the risk of incredulity. Steinzor himself describes it well:

> The ideal of a divorce lived out in friendliness is an attractive
> one, embodying as it does the parents' wish to stop fighting
> and to show the child that though they could not get along
> while married, each parent now wants the child's relation-
> ship to the other to be as good as possible. This approach
> urges on us the reasonableness of brotherly love, of forgetting
> the past, and of salvaging from a sweet dream broken by
> nightmare the fragments that remain warm on awakening.
> Such advice appeals to us because we are all taught in school
> and by our parents to be good sports, to be good losers; after a
> fight we should always shake hands and make up. No argu-
> ment or no difference is so irreconcilable as to make a perma-
> nent rupture.[2]

Steinzor points out that the friendly divorce is coun-
seled by nearly all workers in the field, both in writing
and in counseling practice. Ministers, priests, and rabbis
are especially strong on it because so much of the friendliness ethic springs from religious roots. "Sunday School
behavior" may be a cartoon image in some contexts, but it
also reflects seriously held values, among them the need to
love even enemies, not repay evil with evil, and work toward the other's well-being no matter what he or she has
done. We have gathered all that commitment and more up
in the idea of friendliness, which certainly seems a manageable way to keep the whole ethical package more or less
together, even if the friendship image itself is not originally ethical or theological (you virtually never find it in
the Bible, for instance). If divorcing spouses are managing

[2] Steinzor, p. 23.

at least on the surface to have reasonably friendly dealings with each other, their friends and relatives will almost universally applaud them. No one, by contrast, roots very strongly for people who loathe the idea of having anything to do with their ex-mates.

As a goal for marital ending, however, the friendly divorce, no matter how well vouched for by church and culture, runs smack into three major problems: (1) for most people it is emotionally impossible; (2) it can be harmful for children; and (3) it may derail the necessary emotional process of divorce. I want to talk about each of those difficulties in turn, and then propose another way to look at divorced relations on both psychological and spiritual grounds, something akin to but not quite the same as Steinzor's earlier "divorce with freedom" idea.

Steinzor wrote quite bluntly and categorically,

> I don't think it is possible for a person to live in friendly divorce unless he (sic) is adept at hypocrisy and self-deception, or has left a marriage that has been a friendly, shallow one, short-lived in emotional investment if not in years.[3]

Think about it for a minute. Why should we expect a couple who were not able to get along well enough with each other to sustain a marriage suddenly to be able to be friendly simply because they are no longer married? Or why should we expect parents who had serious reservations about each other's ways of handling the children now to make it a business to support and even praise the ex-spouse to their kids? Or when an unhealthy dependency of one spouse on the other was one of the main things wrong with the marriage, how realistic is it now for the formerly more dominant partner to bind him- or herself to the goal of continuing to "take care of" the person in friendliness when the whole point of the divorce was to eliminate that relationship? To make matters

[3] Steinzor, p. 25.

worse, the actual process of divorce has a potentially healthy way of surfacing buried anger and dissatisfaction so that one can see more clearly why the marriage was irreparably troubled. Most of us would say that is to the good; but it makes the goal of friendliness even more impossible to reach.

In point of fact, one of the commonest problems I see among divorcing people who come for counseling is their difficulty trying to bring off the friendly divorce that their milieu so badly wants them to achieve. One man, for example, ended a marriage of long standing but in the interest of friendliness continually responded to his ex-wife's "emergencies" around the house. The calls for help were the wife's attempts to re-involve him in her own dependency needs, and they left him emotionally exhausted and angry and her bitterly defeated again and again. When it became clear to the man that each of these events could easily have been handled by someone other than himself, conceivably someone who genuinely *was* feeling friendly toward his ex-wife, he experienced an enormous gain in freedom. A woman was relieved to be out of a marriage in which, having put in twenty years as dutiful wife and mother, she could finally acknowledge that she did not love her husband and felt constantly drained and belittled by his crudeness. At the same time, she felt obliged by the myth to be as accommodating as possible to him during the separation period, patiently fending off his attempts to make love to her, enduring his sabotage of her efforts to buy a home of her own, and wearing herself thin telling the children what a good man their father "really" was, among other things. She was paying an enormous price in guilt because of her underlying anger at these antics, to the point that her church participation had dwindled out of sight and the new career on which she had embarked was threatened by her increasing inability to work. The problem was not her anger; it was her long-conditioned attempt to be friendly when that was not at all what she felt or what the situation warranted.

The second difficulty—that the "friendly divorce" may be harmful for children—may come as a surprise, so steeped are we in the idea that pleasantly intimate relationships—even between divorced parents—are the only kind really worthy of positive acclaim. The mischief caused here, though, is emotional hypocrisy, plain and simple. It is one thing for me to be able to acknowledge the positive qualities of a person I otherwise do not especially like; it is something else again for me to try pretend to be that person's champion. The first makes me a decent human being, while the second leaves me a hypocrite. The same is true for parents in divorce. I have found that the children who seem most dedicated to tying their divorcing parents in emotional knots about such things as child support, different disciplinary standards, or who loves whom the most are the children of parents trying for friendly divorce. When the parents themselves call a halt to the mythology, the children rather quickly seem clearer about the whole situation and far better adjusted to it.

The reason is not hard to find. Children are especially keen at picking up lying on the part of grown-ups, and for divorcing parents to maintain a facade of friendliness when the emotional basis for it is not there is a rather clear species of lying. Smaller children may also be mystified, feeling but not being able to express a sense of bewilderment because their unconscious sense of the emotions involved tells them one thing while Mom's or Dad's words are saying something quite contradictory. If we want our children to learn to hide their feelings and not deal as candidly as possible with circumstances as they encounter them, this is one good way to teach them. Richard Gardner, a child psychiatrist who has written helpfully for children of divorce, provides a good illustration of what is at stake. Imagine a father who, having left the marriage, now neglects his young child, does not write or call, visits only sporadically, forgets birthdays, and the like. Mother is quite naturally enraged by such dereliction, while the child is upset and sad. If the mother is committed to the friendly divorce pattern, however, the rules of the game call for her to defend the child's father, no matter how reprehensible his behavior. "You know that your father loves you, dear, but he sometimes is too busy to come by. We just have to understand." I worked with one divorced mother who had bought birthday presents for her children in her ex-husband's name for eleven years rather than let the hard truth surface that their father evidently didn't think them important enough to remember their birthdays. Gardner's advice to parents in this situation is astringent but refreshing. He suggests telling the child that, sad as it is, the father for some reason does not show his love for the child and perhaps does not love the child, and that is a fact we are going to have to adjust to.[4]

The third chief difficulty with the friendly divorce is that it works against the psychological divorcing process, for both parents and children. *Again and again I have found that the best strategy divorcing people can follow is to have as little as possible to do with each other once the separation has occurred.* (The one exception is the fairly rare situation where a carefully structured separation period has been made a part of professionally supervised marital therapy, with explicit objectives and rules.) One objection will now be quickly raised and we had better look at it. "What chance, then, is there for a couple to reconsider and learn that they want to stay married after all if they are not having much of anything to do with each other?" The most honest answer I can give to that question is to say that there is very little chance a couple will reconsider their divorce decision if they are not having much to do

[4] Richard A. Gardner, M.D., *The Boys and Girls Book About Divorce* (Science House, Inc., 1970) p. 19.

with each other, but as these things go there is very little chance they would do so anyway. Moreover, I would argue that it is healthier spiritually and psychologically to learn enough from one failed marriage so that one has an even chance of making a better one in the future than it is to stay enmeshed in a marriage that for very good reasons ought to end. What is happening is that the divorcing process is being sabotaged by the American dream of "never say die" even when it comes to failed marriages.

Here is a subtle and in my view insidious piece of the friendly divorce picture: it sows the seeds of chronic doubt that divorce is ever a permissible, right, or good thing to do. Steinzor more than half suspected that one reason so many of his colleagues prescribed friendly divorce was "perversely punishing them for being antisocial in wanting to divorce."[5] The covert message of the friendly divorce myth is that real, psychological divorce is inappropriate, and that the partners should stay "stuck" with each other emotionally, if not legally, by attempting to achieve in their divorcing relationship what they manifestly could not in their married one. Hence the part of the myth that says, in effect, "If we stay friendly there is a chance we will grow to like each other well enough and repent of this decision to divorce."

What is at issue here is the matter of psychological boundaries, a familiar enough phenomenon in all mental health and relational work but nowhere more critical than in the divorcing situation. For bare survival, let alone healthy relationships, all of us need to be able to recognize, set, and defend what we usually call our personal boundaries. Boundaries are the expectations, rules, standards, and values that reflect who we are as individual human beings, and in turn govern how we will relate to each other. When our boundaries are violated by a person

[5] Steinzor, p. 31.

or a circumstance we feel psychological pain, and if we are healthy we will act to protect what has been broached. All social behavior, including intimate relationships, relies on the establishment and preservation of appropriate personal boundaries. It is one of the most significant things a child has to learn in growing up, and it starts very early on as the infant slowly emerges from its blissful initial narcissism in which the whole world exists only for its immediate gratification. A world of objects—people, events, things—comes slowly into focus and the child learns that all those things, including itself, have shape and definition—starting and stopping places, so to speak, in a word boundaries.

Boundaries govern behavior. We all learn what is acceptable and what is not, what works in one situation but not in another, what one person will tolerate but not everybody will, what we ourselves require for well-being and what we can live without. Boundary-setting is a wide-ranging and never ceasing activity, as picky and mundane as teaching a child that its clothes and toys may not be strewn all over the house, as highly charged as a new lover deciding how close she can allow her significant other to get just now, and as global as achieving self-definition in the face of familial, vocational, or physical threats to the outer perimeter of one's identity.

I do not mean to belabor a concept that is as much a part of our daily lives as food and drink, as well as familiar on professional grounds to most readers. *The point I am making is that one of the things wrong with the friendly divorce is simply that it blurs and confuses boundaries all over the place, for both children and adults, leaving everyone to one degree or another at risk of impairment and dysfunction, as is ever the case when boundaries are under assault.* A divorcing couple is drastically redefining the boundaries of their relationship as spouses and perhaps also as parents, occasionally, too, as work partners and various other roles. There is a lot of pain in that, because boundaries are what serve to keep the chaos of life at bay, and we give up even hateful boundaries only with reluctance. It is imperative when we give up one boundary that we build another at the same time, lest we find ourselves exposed to the psychic elements, so to speak, and thereby imperiled. It is a primitive, basic, and inherently true phenomenon. Divorcing people are in process of forming those new boundaries both for themselves and for their children. *We should take as a basic axiom that anything that interferes with or distorts that forming process is counterproductive to achieving a healthy recovery from the trauma of divorce.* Where the friendly divorce myth works its mischief is precisely here, because it tells people that they should be "bounded together" as friends when in fact what they are trying to do is learn how to bound themselves separately as no-longer-married. Achieving a genuine emotional divorce (what I called "Fifth Divorce" in Chapter One) is a process of redrawing one's relational boundaries from married to single, and what Steinzor doubted was that the process could ever be achieved as long as psychic and social energy were being diverted into the contradictory project of being "friends."

Let me give but one illustration, which will gather up several strands of what we have been talking about. A woman I worked with finally left a philandering husband of many years who was, in my estimation, a charming sociopath. She had been in his thrall in a submissive way until some combination of events and personal development blasted her out of it—not an uncommon circumstance, as Abigail Trafford writes in her useful, bluntly titled book *Crazy Time.*[6] Now as she was wrestling with what I call fourth divorce, she was trying valiantly to be his "friend." Or perhaps it would be better to put it the other way around: trying to stay his friend was what was

---

[6] Abigail Trafford, *Crazy Time: Surviving Divorce* (San Francisco: Harper & Row, 1982).

giving her trouble with fourth divorce. Their separation process was one of the most chaotic I have heard of, partly due to the lethal combination of his craziness and her residual submissiveness. What she had never really learned to do was establish her own boundaries of what was and was not acceptable behavior for her or her children. Visitation was predictably unreliable. Sometimes the husband would do what he had promised with the children and sometimes not. Child support might or might not be forthcoming. One phone call between the two would be filled with affection, while the next would be a screaming match, and so on it went. The dominant value my client was working with was friendliness; she was almost willing to set her own well-being and identity as a person aside in order to try to be friends with her estranged husband, and it was draining her emotional reserves rather rapidly. To use a metaphor, what was happening was that whenever she succeeded in drawing a boundary about her own needs or her children's behavior or her living schedule, her disruptive husband would attempt to breach it, and her drive toward friendliness would not only *let* it happen but baptize it in the name of how things were supposed to be. Only as she came to realize that drawing boundaries is not unfriendly could she give up the myth, and that is a dynamic to which I now wish to turn—an alternative to the friendly divorce.

So far this section has been empty of my own experience, for the basic reason that the myth of friendly divorce has been something I myself have struggled long and hard with. I am, after all, a Christian pastor, and trying to be kind is near the top of the list of things I seek to embody in my own spiritual odyssey. Years ago, before my own marriage was at least consciously in jeopardy, I read Steinzor's book and used it enthusiastically in my counseling practice. His lean advice to get away clean, so to speak, and be responsible without trying to be friendly made as much sense then as it does to me now. When it came time to negotiate the treacherous waters of my own divorce, however, I came to some heavy going.

My wife and I had worked hard at the marriage and were then working equally hard at the divorce. "Damage control," I believe it is called in naval circles when a ship has been attacked. Our aim was to get the job done with as little disruption as possible, for the boys' sakes as well as our own. We were grateful, and still are, that at least we were not suffering from the acrimony and suspicious secrecy that seemed to surround so many of the divorced people we knew. I did not want a "friendly divorce," but neither did I want to be unkind or uncaring. I did not love my wife anymore in the way one would have to to sustain a marriage, and there were times when in my fantasy I could cheerfully have throttled her for not being the kind of person I had tried to make her be! But even then I took seriously the difference between *getting divorced* (as a state one finally achieves) and *divorcing* (as a process that, technically speaking, never ends for a once-married couple, especially when children are involved), and I accepted in my heart that I would always have some sort of connection to this woman, which in turn would mean that I would always be willing to care about and for her as best I could within the limits appropriate to our situation as divorced people.

I confess I probably tried for the friendly divorce for a time, even while I was arguing consciously and vocally for "divorce with freedom." Slowly, though, a distinction began to emerge, to my great relief, and it is the note on which I want this section to end. It happened while working with my anger—which was immense. I kept wanting to be kind, decent, responsible, honest, and the signals that kept coming from my upbringing and from my culture, especially its religious part, was that that meant being *friendly*. At the same time I was all too acutely aware just how wounded and angry I was, and that was most assuredly not "friendly." Then one day "the penny dropped," so to speak, and I realized that what I wanted had a far better image than friendliness; I wanted simply to be *civilized*.

Now it came clear what had always bothered me about the concept of divorce with freedom as an alternative to the friendly divorce myth. Without friendliness the relational landscape looked pretty inhospitable. Divorcing with freedom sounded antiseptic, if not downright mean by comparison. Did it mean we cut off all ties and responsibilities and stalked away in self-righteousness? Of course not. Did it mean we hung up the phone briskly whenever the ex-spouse called, or declined any request for information or assistance? No, I couldn't accept that. Freedom surely was not meanness or even quarantine. What was it, then?

Years ago I came across one of those funky epigrams that you find turned into calligraphy or needlepoint and can never quite find a place to display. As imperfectly as I remember it, it read something like, "If a man first indulges himself in murder, he will soon come to think nothing of robbery; then he will decline to lying, [and so on through a long list] until he is finally reduced to procrastination and incivility." Here was what I was searching for. My closely held values of kindness, decency, responsibility, and honesty added up to what I would from then on call *civility*, and the difference between that and "friendship" as the myth used it was simply immense. The trick was that friendship as an image and a goal involved a blurring of boundaries in the divorce situation, while civility did not. Civility was a different animal altogether; it implied no particular kind of relationship, bondedness, or commitment to the other beyond what the concept itself implied, namely that anyone who sought to act it out would be as kind, decent, responsible, and honest as possible. *Civility establishes a code of interaction, not a relationship.* That is the key distinction. That famous poetic line of Frost's comes to mind, "Good fences make good neighbors." It was meant partly in irony, but also in deep earnest. It is only when boundaries are clear and adequately protected that neighborliness flourishes, for the psychologically basic reason that it is only when our individual selves are adequately defined and protected against the onslaughts of outer chaos that we are able to enter into relationships of *any* kind—marrying or divorcing or any point in between. Civility may or may not lead to friendship; with divorcing people it probably will not, and all to the good. It may, however, lead to a clarity and leanness of interaction that on spiritual and religious grounds is the sort of thing gathered up again and again in religious thinking as peace, *shalom.* Civility is a great respecter and cultivator of boundaries, whatever they may be, and it is what gave "freedom" the dimension of humaneness it had not quite had before in my thinking.

Now at last I was comfortable with an alternative to the friendly divorce. *What we would seek was divorce with freedom, nurtured through boundary-respecting civility.* Whether we are angry or happy, fighting or cooperating, working toward a common end or seeking our own welfare, it is possible to seek divorce with civility. No, it will not always be easy; and no, civility is certainly not an insulating blanket to throw over the strong feelings of the experience. But I offer it as a better way than the friendly divorce myth of putting into some spiritually and theologically acceptable perspective the complicated and emotion-laden process of divorce. Think of it as a kind of compass for the journey, perhaps.

It is for another time and place to apply this rethinking to our approach to ministry with divorcing people. Here suffice it to say that the church's pastoral care would go a lot further toward both meeting people's needs and embodying the love of which the Gospel speaks if it could help divorcing people understand the difference between *shalom*, as I have described it, and the, by comparison, anemic secular image of "friendliness." People in great pain have a remarkably low tolerance for emotional dishonesty. Too often, I fear, the price the church has put on its ministry for people experiencing the pain of divorce is acceptance of this emotional deceit of the friendly divorce, and they flee from us because deep down they *know* it is a sham. Either that, or they are irretrievably weighed down by guilt at not being able to do what they mistakenly believe—and what the church too often encourages them to believe—is necessary on theological grounds to be both divorcing and acceptable in God's eyes.

When we shift our thinking toward making peace instead of being friends, we come a step closer to a more explicitly spiritual and theological way of talking. To one of the most misunderstood, troublesome, but potentially helpful concepts in the Judaeo-Christian tradition we now turn.

THREE

Reconciliation May Not Be What You Think

"RECONCILIATION" is a word you hear a lot about both in religious circles and in marital separation and divorce. It is one of the few terms I know that seems to be both thoroughly theological and thoroughly secular, with roughly the same meaning in either setting. Being a divorcing clergyman therefore gave me a double dose of it, and it was not easy.

My own separation came about after months of agonizing effort on both my wife's and my parts to be "responsible" both in and out of marriage counseling. That in turn had been preceded by years of worry and work on a relationship that, in the best hindsight I can muster, was doomed almost from the beginning. With the actual separation therefore came an almost euphoric burst of newly freed energy. Yes, I was deeply hurt and torn in a dozen different directions, scared, lonely, guilt-ridden, and all the rest. But this separation was no impetuous flinging away from each other; it had been achingly chiseled out, and the relief I felt now that it was accomplished was simply enormous. One day not long after it had happened, a teaching colleague asked solicitously how I was getting along. He was an older minister, more conservative than I, one of the gentlest and most caring people around. The idea of divorce, particularly among clergy, was, I imagine, upsetting to him. After we had exchanged a few words walking along, he stopped, lowered his voice, and asked earnestly, "Is there any chance of a reconciliation?" Anyone observing us would have seen and heard no more than my brief reply, stern-faced, "No, I don't think so."

What I was feeling *inside*, however, I am grateful was not on public view. I was almost laughing, saying to myself, "My God! If you only knew how much hard work it took to get *out* of that marriage! No way in hell would I want to go back into the fray and lose it all." I knew what my colleague intended, of course, and I was moved by his concern, which is probably what gave me enough unexpected self-control to keep what I was thinking to myself. Much later my lawyer asked me exactly the same question, and part of the ritual legal language of the divorce itself required him to announce to the court that there was no possibility of a reconciliation.

And so, both theologically and socially, those of us who divorce have failed at reconciliation, publicly struck out. Somehow the kindliness with which that obvious judgment is passed these days made it sting even more—sufficiently so that I quietly began to wonder if it was even *right*. As time went by I grew convinced that in fact it was not, and that is the subject of this chapter. When I am through I will be saying that contrary to what our popular idea has been, reconciliation has taken place, and can for thousands of divorcing people who are now clogging the lists of the unreconciled failures at marriage.

Reconciliation does not at first seem to be such a difficult concept, in either theological or everyday use. We assume it means an end of conflict and differences, and the establishment of an agreeable and positive relationship. Maritally speaking, it means that the rupture of separation, either physical or emotional, has been repaired and a couple is back together again on good terms. The picture of reconciliation most of us carry in our heads is therefore something like joining hands again, united in newly established commonality.

What I have come to believe, however, is that that is not what reconciliation means at all, and that our slightly romantic picture is simply wrong. To begin with, reconciliation is a concept that comes from the Bible, and the Bible is just not a very democratic or romantic document. The biblical meaning of the concept is nothing like holding hands and walking into the sunset. *Reconciliation means instead putting an end to mutual destructiveness and hostility.* It signifies the beginning of what in modern terms we might call a new "contract" among people in which something has happened so that they are not killing each other anymore. The boundaries of a relationship have been redrawn, in other words, so that destruction ceases. That is "reconciliation."

The important thing to see is that such reconciliation can take many forms. It may, true enough, mean a new "joining" together; *but it may also mean a conflict-free agreement to go our separate ways in peace.* It may mean agreeing to disagree; it may mean fighting hard—but justly—for hon-

estly held differences of conviction; it may mean giving up
sadistic pleasure in fighting and retiring to separate cor-
ners. The essence of the thing is the end to the mutual
destruction, the recontracting of personal boundaries so
they are no longer on a war footing. Whatever arrangement works toward achieving these goals is in service to
reconciliation, on biblical, spiritual grounds. That is precisely what happens when a bad marriage ends and a
"good" divorce, anchored in peace and civility, takes its
place. Oftentimes, in other words, divorce is a way of
reaching reconciliation.

To some that will come as a new or perhaps unbelievable notion. What has happened, after all, to the friendliness, the warm feeling, the camaraderie, the love that we
have associated with reconciliation? The answer is simply
that it was never there to begin with *so far as the meaning of
reconciliation itself is concerned.* We added those ingredients
to the idea, romanticized it if you please, for the perfectly
understandable reason that some forms of reconciliation
do indeed also carry with them good and loving feelings.
Some forms, but not *all:* that is the point.

The "additives" never had anything to do with the basic
concept, but over a period of time confusion set in. It
might be helpful to know, for instance, that the Greek
word the New Testament uses as "reconciliation" in clas-
sical times originally meant simply "exchange," as in the
exchange of money. That continues to be its meaning in
theological terms: the exchange of destructiveness for a
new relationship that is not destructive, "thereby bringing
the hostility to an end," as it is explained in Ephesians
2:16. Even the only time Jesus himself uses the word has
nothing to do with feelings, but rather with establishing a
nondestructive contract with one's brother or sister (Mt.
5:24).

It should also be clear that a living arrangement alone
has as little to do with the heart of reconciliation as feel-

ings of warmth or affection. To use both extremes, it is quite possible for long-divorced people not to have achieved reconciliation because they are still, in effect, living and acting destructively toward each other, whether deliberately or not; and it is equally possible for once separated couples who have gotten back together again and seem "reconciled" in the social-arrangements sense not to be any closer to real reconciliation than when they started. Reconciling in this sense is a process, sometimes quite a long one. What I am trying to push for here is our seeing reconciling as a process that goes along with divorcing, may for some people even be synonymous with it, rather than the popular view of it as one that, by definition, undoes divorcing.

Let me illustrate this whole way of thinking with a brief case study of rethinking reconciliation in a nonmarital situation. Not long ago I was called on by a group of ministers to lead them in a sort of group-therapy retreat in response to a devastating experience they had had. A member of their group had pled guilty to charges of sexual abuse of children in his congregation after a year of stoutly maintaining his innocence. The minister colleagues felt betrayed, used, lied to, and a whole host of other complicated things. They were trying but largely failing to put the whole matter behind them and get on with their life and work. What they wanted, they said, was help in coming to some reconciliation in the whole sordid business—reconciliation with their colleague, who had resigned from the ministry, and to a lesser extent reconciliation with each other over the differences of feeling and opinion many of them had had during the past year or so in which the incident had been most volatile. They were trying to balance their Christian duty to love and care for their brother and his family with their anger and hurt at having been used and sold out by his behavior, and particularly by his consistent lying. The felonious member was keeping things stirred up and manipulated by reappearing on the scene from time to time even after he had resigned and before his imprisonment was to begin.

You must understand that nothing in this world can so tie a group of ministers in knots as having to love, forgive, and be reconciled to a fellow minister whom they could cheerfully and for cause have throttled. Or to put it differently, turning an unrepentant sociopath loose among a group of loving Christians bent on forgiveness is a little like setting the fox amongst the chickens. The trouble they were having with reconciliation was the same trouble divorcing people often have: they did not understand that properly understood reconciliation redraws and redefines boundaries rather than blurring them in a great, loving embrace that tries to deny the real destructiveness going on. To achieve reconciliation meant, in this instance, acknowledging that their colleague had by his behavior and his overt choice placed himself beyond the pale. They would find reconciliation not by finding ways to keep "loving" him and associating with him, but rather by just the opposite: divorcing themselves from him and clarifying that he was no longer within the boundaries of their association. Once they could get over what initially seemed the harshness of that, they were able to see that in fact this is what reconciliation meant all along. In a somewhat paradoxical way, they were free to be mutually *for* their colleague only after they had acknowledged and clarified the end of his relationship with them.

Let me return to the story with which I began this chapter. If I were able to replay the encounter with my minister friend, I would do it much differently. I would like to be able to reply something like this to his question whether reconciliation was possible: "Yes, Sam, it is possible and that is what we are working on now. We have decided that in this most basic, spiritual sense we cannot be reconciled so long as we are married. We have separated in order to achieve reconciliation, for our and our children's sakes, and though it is a process which is not complete yet, we are making good, though painful, progress. In time we will make it, and the destructiveness that our married relationship sadly created will not exist in our new relationship—which is what it is, all right—as divorcing people."

In that reply I would be saying three things. One is that the end of a marriage does not necessarily or maybe even possibly mean the end of a relationship between the former spouses. It will be a divorcing relationship, and in time there will hopefully be absolutely no contact between the two at all. But one of the odd things that seldom gets talked about in the subject of divorce is that, particularly after a long marriage, the former partners, no matter how "well" divorced, remain in a certain kind of relationship, at least on historical and emotional grounds. I have yet to meet a divorced person whose life did not at least in some degree include a sense of relationship to his or her former spouse, and I am thinking now of what I would regard as the healthy situations where the marriage has well and truly ended across-the-board, not the troubled ones where the ex-mates are still in some undesirable ways hooked into each other. Divorce brings a radical *change* in relationship, but apparently not a complete end of it. We may wish it were different, but in the parts of the human drama I have witnessed thus far, it does not seem to be in the script. The question therefore is whether my divorcing relationship can be a more reconciling one than my married relationship was, in the sense of ending mutual destructiveness. I would want my friend to see that.

A second thing is that while we acknowledged we had failed to make the marriage we wanted, we were not accepting the label of "failure" at being responsible, loving human beings. Part of the inescapable grief in divorce comes from having to acknowledge that at the very least we have lost the dream once held for what that marriage might be; we have failed to bring it off, for whatever reasons. There is failure enough in divorce, God knows, and I believe divorcing people have a right to claim the area of reconciliation as one in which they do *not* fail. There is an ironic sense in which if I have been able to sever connections and stop flailing my former spouse, to give up that destructive agenda, then I can credit myself with having succeeded at something important, and politely decline society's label of "failure" at reconciliation.

The third thing is that reconciliation is not an end in itself, even on biblical, theological grounds, but only a means to the end of being able to love again. When energy that was locked up by destructiveness is released in reconciliation, it is available to be invested, and *that* is the objective, whether one sees it in explicitly religious or more broadly spiritual terms. Working with divorcing people, I notice a certain turning point somewhere in the process that seems crucially important but is often missed. It happens when the motivation for ending a marriage shifts from *flight* to *reinvestment*, when a person is propelled not so much by the need to get away from a painful situation as by the desire to give him or herself in new ways that a failing marriage is making impossible: to children, to other friends, to work, to one's own growth and development, eventually to a new lover. Divorcing people who do not reach that turning point tend to remain, in my experience, embittered, sad, and locked into mourning for lost dreams. People who are able to reach it and go beyond are also quite entitled to anger, sadness, and grieving, but the trajectory of it, so to speak, is different. It is like the difference between withdrawing my money from a sour investment and putting it into something more promising rather than stuffing it fearfully under the mattress. We would do far better in helping divorcing people if we saw reconciliation as a means to reaching that turning point even in and through divorce.

We can return briefly here to the previous chapter's subject, and the mischief done by the stereotype of the "friendly divorce." Perhaps one source of that enduring myth is our misconception of reconciliation. Because we have thought that once divorced we had by definition failed at reconciliation, we may have sought to salvage at least something that the social and religious world would approve of by being "friendly." Keep in mind that the popular image of reconciliation was not too far from "friendliness." Perhaps the friendly divorce was the best we could come up with as a pinch hit for what we mistakenly thought of as real reconciliation we could not achieve. Ironically, of course, exactly the reverse may be true, as I was arguing earlier: couples who are locked into a destructive interaction because they are striving against impossible odds to be friends are not only not making up for a failure at reconciliation but are rather actively making matters much worse.

If we give up the myth of the friendly divorce and aim, as I am hoping, for civility and peacemaking, then reconciliation can become a goal of the divorcing process. In fact, the kind of freedom from interaction we strive for in a "civilized" divorce will do far more for the end of destructiveness than the impossibly mixed messages of the friendly divorce. It will take different shapes in different situations, and to some of those differences I now want to turn.

I am aware that in order to try to be clear about my point, I have so far been talking as though the divorcing partners were working more or less equally hard at the process. There is no doubt that things go better when that is the case, but unfortunately it seldom is the case in the real world. What do you do, then, when your former spouse is playing the game by different rules? I am thinking now of two broad categories of situation, one in which one spouse persists in destructiveness, and another in which one spouse with a seemingly more positive motivation wants to keep the relationship friendly or even revive the marriage. (Sometimes, of course, the two categories coexist in one person, which can give us a Jekyll and Hyde situation that adds its own brand of anguish.) Both are out-of-balance situations and both are painful.

In the first case reconciling behavior is going to seem very odd, particularly if you are a person with strong ethical or religious commitments to forgiveness, loving even your enemies, and the like. Here reconciling is best served by drawing firm, clear boundaries and enforcing them with every resource in your power—including, if necessary, the appropriate public authorities and the courts. It will be a double struggle: to keep the destructiveness of a former spouse out of your life, but also to keep your anger and wish for retribution out of his or hers. A boundary, in other words, fences both in and out, a tidy distinction we often overlook. Roger was a man in his fifties who had left his wife Meryl of nearly thirty years and there was nothing mutual about the decision. She had suffered a mild stroke several years before, and part of Roger's guilt at leaving a woman not exactly sick but not completely her old self either stemmed from a years-long battle with his tendency to "rescue" her and her tendency to become dependent on him—one of the things that had eventually brought the marriage to an end. Roger was a kind person with strong Christian convictions about caring for other people, the very sort of person who often finds it hardest to enforce boundaries. In her rage at being left, Meryl developed the pattern of calling Roger with the veiled but unmistakable message that she was considering suicide. He would rush over to the house, sometimes to find her hail and hearty, sometimes not to find her at all, and at least once to find her comatose, apparently from an overdose. Each time he would be pulled back into her world, and the outcome was another round of bitter fighting, recriminations exchanged, and remorse. It was like cranking up an old play, and every time he walked on stage he picked up his cues and played his part to perfection. The boundary he needed to draw was simple to describe but very tough to enforce. He had to realize that while his former wife might indeed need help even of an emergency nature, he was not the person who could give it to her. He was coached to tell Meryl that he would not under any circumstances come to her aid, though he would call the rescue squad if she wanted him to, and if the emergency people found her not in need of help after all, that would be her problem to unravel. Predictably, the "drama" soon ended, though not without a struggle on Roger's part to keep himself from responding to Meryl's call for help, particularly under the onslaught of her accusations of his ruthlessness, un-Christian callousness, and lack of love. The boundaries had to be drawn more or less unilaterally, and while it was unpleasant for everyone it was also "reconciling."

When young children are involved, boundary-setting can be even more complicated. One of the most painful situations arises when an ex-spouse uses the children, consciously or not, as a weapon against the former partner, perhaps by overtly telling them what a rotten person their other parent is, or perhaps more subtly, using them as message bearers to shame, chastise, or cajole the other. Marianne's eight-year-old son called from his father's house to invite her for dinner, at the father's instigation, and it was terribly difficult for her to draw the boundary with the child that it was his father's, not his, place to extend such an invitation. Perhaps it was even harder for her to refuse it, but it was necessary that she do so. John's young teenagers were forever asking him to buy them clothes because "Mom just doesn't have any money." John was a responsible provider, gave adequate child support to his ex-wife, and knew that though finances were not easy for either of them, the fact was she had enough money for the children's regular clothes, as they had agreed she would. He also knew that his former wife's complaining to the children about lack of money was a way of complaining about him. What he had to tell the children, not without difficulty, was that he and their mother had agreed that their clothes would be her expense and he provided child support for that purpose. If he took them shopping, he expected to be reimbursed promptly by their mother.

Children's reactions are marvelous ways of determining how you are doing with the matter of boundaries, simply because they are always naturally testing them and pouring through any breach they find like water through a hole in the dam. It can be infuriating, heartbreaking, and comic; it can also be usefully instructive. I firmly believe that the best protection for children from harm in divorce is clarity and reliability in the boundaries of the relationship between parents and among parents and children. Damage is done by confusion on the boundaries, children not knowing *quite* what to expect of whom under what circumstances because it keeps changing. Martha could not shed her guilt over "destroying the family" by leaving a marriage riddled by her husband's chronic and unrepentant adultery, and matters were not being helped by frequent comments from the children about how much they missed being a family together. Martha was also vacillating back and forth in her dealings with her estranged husband, at least thinking about if not actually doing such things as having him for dinner, arranging "family" outings, taking the kids to visit his parents, and the like. Her interpretation of the situation was that the children's pressure to be a family again kept the boundaries blurred about what relationship she wanted with their father. My interpretation was the reverse: that her confusion about the boundaries was picked up by the children, who responded predictably by feeding her ambivalence through their comments. When she took herself rather forcefully in hand, decided that interactions with the former husband had to be pared to the minimum necessary for child-rearing business, and told the children plainly that mommy and daddy were not getting back together again, all complaints vanished and the children flourished.

Martha's is really a situation of the second broad type, where an ex-spouse apparently wants to be friendly and to stay inappropriately involved. The difficulty with boundary-setting here is that it is awfully easy for you to look like the bad guy, certainly in the eyes of a society that puts a premium on reconciliation of the re-joining type and the friendly divorce. I am afraid, though, that biting the bullet is the only solution, and here I offer a perspective on that which allows such a firm response to be seen as consistent with the positive values of reconciliation and other-serving mutuality. I remember a time in my own experience when my former wife and I decided it was time to prepare for sale the house where she and the children still lived. The boys were scheduled to be with me that weekend, but we all pitched in for a whirlwind day of cleanup at the house, and rather than they and I leaving to go back to my place for the evening, I invited her to come for dinner, which I had prepared in advance. It seemed simply a decent thing to do, since we were all tired, my meal was all but done, and she would otherwise have had to fix something for herself alone.

It was a mistake. I should not have offered and she should not have accepted. We had crossed the line from the civility we were trying, more or less successfully, to put into practice over into friendliness, and the evening hung thickly with mixed messages, unexpressed anger, and freshly scratched sadness. Because that evening, to its own small degree, put us back into the soup rather than helping us differentiate ourselves, it went against the grain of reconciliation, even though most people "outside" would have applauded it as a model thing to do.

This chapter accomplishes two things, really, one reassuring and the other perhaps mildly inflammatory. On the reassuring side, I want those of us who are divorcing and trying to maintain a pattern of responsibility based on spiritual commitments to see even our ending marriages as potentially a form of what both the theological and secular worlds value so highly, reconciliation. The word "potentially" means, of course, that we have to be willing to identify and then to give up our own destructiveness, which is never an easy task. My hope is that we will find it more manageable once we are also freed of the burden of the friendly divorce myth, so that the alternative to destruction does not have to be coziness.

On the inflammatory side, we who are divorcing have both room and responsibility to say as forcefully as we can to the church, to our associates, to families, and to society that reconciliation is not reserved for the happily together, and that we want to claim it, too, to be judged by our own behavior. On the other hand, I myself have seen too many marriages in which some sort of armed truce has been reached, leaving the partners unable to extend themselves in love or concern to anyone or anything else, so caught up are they in maintaining a tense status quo. If these unions have been certified as "reconciliation," I think it is time their license was revoked. The concept reaches too deeply and importantly into the human spirit for us to tolerate its abuse, and perhaps that is a message those of us who know firsthand the ache of divorce have to give.

FOUR

*Promises, Promises,
Always Promises*

I IMAGINE you have seen one version or another of the rather bad cartoon in which a couple getting married exchange their vows not with the traditional words "till death do us part" or "as long as we both shall live" but with something like "until this relationship loses its meaningfulness." It is meant, obviously, as a dig at the pop-psych language that sometimes took the place of more standard religious commitment, especially during the 1960s. Once I may have found those cartoons amusing; I do not anymore. For people like me whose commitments are supported by what we at least hope are spiritual and religious values, being reminded that in divorce we have at least in some fashion "broken our vows" is one of the most painful parts of the whole business.

Here I am talking especially to two very different but also very closely related kinds of people: one, the divorcing person who is worried and perhaps feels guilty about the violation of his or her marriage vows, and two, the hurt and angry divorcing spouse who either feels that those vows have been broken against their desire and will, or who realizes that they *could* have held on and endured a bad marriage but chose not to. The violator and the violated, perhaps. The reason I have not done the simple thing and divided the chapter into two sections, one for each audience, is that I believe each needs to hear what is said to the other, because at the end of the day it may just be that all of us are a little of both.

I cannot hide my own ambivalence on the subject. On the one hand, I know, as I will be saying more about a bit later, that a wedding vow establishes a commitment to a relationship, a hope if you please, but that it does not automatically and magically before the fact supersede all other values and unforeseen events. But at the same time there is that solemn sense of a lifetime covenant, entered into in the sight of God, as most of us said, which seems to threaten unspeakable consequences, something on the order of annihilation of integrity, if not of being itself, if it is sundered. In the end the only thing that holds that conflict together for me and keeps it from being overwhelming is the image that it is not so much a breaker of promises that I look at in the mirror as it is a broken human being. And then begins to dawn some deep, visceral realization of what it means to hear, in theological terms familiar to most more or less religious people, that God joins me in my brokenness and seeks to restore me to my spiritual journey. But that is the end of the story; several other things must come first.

When I was separated, an old and dear friend with whom I frequently corresponded asked whether divorce was not particularly hard for a clergyman, what with the theological weight of those wedding vows hanging so heavily in my commitment. I recently reread my reply to her and was startled at how angry and self-righteous it was, testimony, I now think, to my guilt and shame too easily exposed by a simple question. What about the vows? I wrote that I had dreamed the answer, such as it was. In the dream I am part of a wedding party, one of several clergy who will conduct the service like a Greek chorus, each one with a part to say. Mine is the last, the vows, and when the time comes I miss my cue. It has to be done over, but I have lost my place in the book, and make something up instead. There is one word I am supposed to say, though I cannot remember for sure what it was, something like "depend." Instead I prattle on about flowers, symbolic meanings of a vivid picture, perhaps the bride's dress, gobbledygook that is poetic and lovely until someone objects that there are no vows. *"How can this couple be married without vows?"* Feverishly, not much time left now, I page through my book to find the place. When I do find it I discover to my horror that there are no vows there—they have been cut out. I borrow another book, into which my missing pages have been mysteriously pasted. Relief! Until I read them and see that this particular service *has no vows in it.* The couple in the dream turn out to be old friends, divorced in actual fact not long after they were married in real, waking life.

If my conscious mind believed it had no problem with wedding vows, my dreaming unconscious easily proved otherwise. My dream was expressing the wish that the marriage had never really happened, that there had been no vows. Perhaps in some deep psychological sense that in fact was true: the marriage had somehow not really happened. But is that so different, I wrote my friend back then, from saying, as I even had to my former wife, that I would give anything if it were not the way it is and if I had been able to love in the way I could not by the end?

How are we to think about this affront we have apparently caused at least to society and possibly to God? All too often the thinking is plainly magical, and I believe we can do far better than that, which is the purpose of this chapter. It is a curious thing, but the only times I have ever heard married people give any indication of even *thinking* about their wedding vows are on special anniversaries *and in divorce*. It is almost as though they were un-self-consciously there in the marriage, like a vaccination received long ago and hopefully still doing its protective work without any outward signs whatever. When the marriage hits trouble we wonder, sometimes with agony, what happened to that protection, set in place so ceremoniously amidst white satin, flower petals, and terminal anxiety? What was a vow anyway? What does it mean that either we or it or both have failed now?

I am seeing in my mind's eye the stricken look on the faces of divorcing people who say with a mixture of anger and incredulous sadness, "But what about those vows we took? Are they all for nothing?" The promises are broken now, but what worries me is the feeling I sense that somehow *these* promises were supposed to have been immune from the human brokenness that all of us share as a common spiritual legacy. That is the magical flavor I speak of here, the sense almost that the language of the marriage rite could or should have insulated us from the often horrifying reality of being human. A wounded innocence surrounds people who feel this way, adding its own ingredient to the already complex mixture of divorce pain. We feel doubly betrayed—by the wife or husband who did not measure up, but also by those incredible words we said, oh so long ago, which did not after all possess the magical power we hoped they did, without realizing it, to keep at bay the plain reality of divorce. I remember now, with a mixture of sadness and offense, the words of the minister who performed my own marriage. He is a beloved friend to this day, but even then his bantering comment just before the service, "You realize that weddings I perform are guaranteed not to come undone" felt hollow, spooky, gone off, with the unmistakable smell of magic in the air. What I am trying to say here is that in genuinely religious terms such magic has no place, because it keeps us away from the only thing that gives religious value any currency in the first place, namely the encounter with and transcendence of human brokenness in all its forms. The part of divorce that can be spiritual journey is just this experience of brokenness and eventually healing, this coming face-to-face with the fact that I was not after all protected by an envelope of magical words but rather that I tried my best, failed, and for all that am neither destroyed nor worthless in the eyes of God.

I am talking here about not only the sense of *violation* in those for whom that term literally applies, but also about the sense of *failure* in those who, behaviorally speaking, are blameless. Here is a woman, for instance, whose unrepentantly philandering and undependable husband would happily have continued the marriage—on his terms. So far as actual behavior goes he is the one who could be said to have violated the vows. She chose to end the marriage, on grounds few people would have anything but sympathy for. She realizes all this, and can even articulate that in a dominant sense her vows were broken *for her* by her husband. Yet even in her position there is that nagging "for better or worse" clause that leaves her wondering whether she *should* have endured the worst. Her decision not to rests uneasily with her not as violation of vows but as failure to sustain them, and she represents a large number of the people I am trying to talk to now.

We first learn about broken promises not as marriage partners but as children, when what someone who loved us promised did not happen. If we are lucky we experience tolerable degrees of that betrayal, learning in the process that there are reasons for it which do not leave the very idea of a promise bankrupt. Children can become quite adept—far more so than their parents, I am convinced—at telling which promises have a realistic chance of making it and which are doomed from birth. They learn to believe in and rely on the former, and take the rest with either a good-humored or furious grain of salt, but a grain nonetheless. If we are unlucky we come to distrust the world and grow up unable to put our faith in any kind of promise or commitment, our own or anyone else's. Few of us, thank God, are so blighted, but in divorce at least some version of the child's question surfaces, "Can I afford to trust at all again? If this promise collapsed under the weight my partner and I put on it, will any other fare better?"

What we learn about promises as children some of us relearn as young parents, and this brings us closer to the subject of vows in marriage and divorce. I am quite sure that I was more disturbed than my young children when I discovered that I could not keep all my promises to them, not even some of the ordinary, easy ones. All the pressures of the workaday world, coupled with my own venality, conspired against the idealism of the young father who, like most such creatures, was doing no more than pursuing the dream of innocence lost in childhood when he vowed to himself never, ever to break a promise to his kids. The first unavoidable business conflict, the first unvarnished forgetfulness, the first change of heart changed all that. My younger son unwittingly gave us a code for the process, which added a grace note of humor to the disappointment of unkept bargains. We frequently drove by a rather interesting-looking restaurant called The Foolish Fox, which I had never been in but knew to be your basic fairly swanky bar with food on the side. At about age four or five Adam asked whether we could go to eat there, and I, having learned my lesson about such things by now, replied, "Someday we will." Every time we passed the place I could expect the question from the other side of the car, "Dad, when are we going to The Foolish Fox?" "Oh, someday," I would ritually reply. Soon, however, the child caught on, and began to come back with "Dad, when is 'someday'?" This went on for years, until I finally overcame what frankly had been my own anxiety and took the child to The Foolish Fox—for a very pleasant meal, as it turned out. Long before that, however, the code had developed: to every request for a commitment about which I was queasy, I would just reply "someday," to a predictable chorus of derisive, laughing jeers about what "someday" meant in Dad's strange lexicon. Yes, we all laughed; but I confess here that a part of me did not laugh, the part that was heartbroken because I could not be a better father to my kids, could not be any more than human even on the best of days.

What, though, does this little excursion through my reminiscence as a parent have to do with the broken vows of marriage? First, it reminds me that on the evidence of broken promises *alone* no score can be tallied about my worth or effectiveness as a parent. It depends on how I handle those betrayals, on what was at stake in them, on how well I integrate them into an overall pattern of love and trustworthiness as a parent on all the other grounds available to me. Being a parent is a complicated business, as those of you who have tried it know, and global judgments about success or failure based on limited pieces of the parenting experience are always risky.

The same is true, I believe, in marriage and divorce.

Any marriage is full of broken promises, most of them nonfatal, forgivable, even laughable. When I have to come face-to-face with breaking the supposedly "unbreakable" vow of the marriage, it may be that I confront my own weakness, sinfulness, or mistakenness, but I want to say that I do not in that moment confront a total judgment on my worth as a marriage partner, still less as a total person. I find myself instead at a way station on the journey, one full of misery and recrimination, much of it self-inflicted, some of it thrown in by family, friends, the church, or society. The important thing is that I am somehow able to look at my-promising-self realistically rather than magically.

The other thing that vignette about my children speaks to is more far-reaching, and leads to one of the main themes of this chapter. What all those promises to my children, some kept and some broken, added up to was not establishing myself as a more or less reliable quartermaster but rather *establishing a relationship as a parent.* Though never much talked about in the open, that was the real "work" being done by parental promising, aside from the specific content of this or that agreement. The underlying, unstated, but supremely important "promise" was that I would be their father, that I would hold their best interests paramount, and that to the best of my ability I would not lie to them—even about my inability to keep each and every promise—or mislead them or use them to my own ends. Success or failure as a parent did not come from the box score of promises kept and broken, but from how well I—and, not insignificantly, *they* too—did at building the relationship. It was a relationship with its pluses and minuses, successes and failures, ups and downs, but for all that it was a steady, continuous interconnectedness that made us parent and children, and the promising was really a tool, among others, in its building.

The same is true for marriage: what is important even

beyond the explicit content of the vow is the underlying meaning that two people have committed themselves to building a relationship. That relationship will inevitably change as the years go by. That is normal and healthy; few of us, I daresay, would want it to be the same twenty years later as it was on our wedding days. When some of us come to the point of divorce we are forced to acknowledge that the change has become so radical we cannot be married anymore. The commitment to a process that those vows inaugurated has failed, but what has to be more clearly said than I often hear is that the vow never was, especially in a religious sense, a binding, rock-solid forecast of the future. It was a commitment to doing something that now has failed. I would go so far as to say, at the risk of sounding sophistic, that all vows change because all relationships change, and the essential *work* of a vow is the establishment of relationship, not the ordering up of a result. The "change" of divorce is radical and final; it signals the end of the process of building one kind of relationship (and the beginning of the process of building another), but apart from the severity of the change, what has happened is no different from what happens with any vow, even those that look for all the world to have been "kept."

"Relationship" is probably too overused a word these days, too easily diluted. We need to know its opposite to regain some of its significance, and the way that comes to me best to do that is to tell the following story. A counseling client of mine is in the painful process of ending a friendship and trying to figure out why. His friend was a person who had been a unique combination of colleague, student, friend, and lover, who in the best moments was competent, effervescent, supportive, full of light and the naive innocence of discovering more about the world than it had ever before unfolded. But here, too, was a person whose mood and commitment to the friendship could change like quicksilver, and who in the end could not be counted on to *be there*, particularly if the relationship made any demands, as all relationships by definition do. What was frustrating to my client was not being able to find any pattern, anything in their interaction that could account for his friend's sudden changes in commitment. It was the *not knowing why* that hurt as much as her flinging away. After months of trying to puzzle out why this friendship could not seem to "stick," including a lot of soul-searching and self-examination of his own, in which he identified and owned some of the strains he had put on their relationship, the answer suddenly appeared. His friend is a person who for some understandable reasons of personal background lives a life of *episodes* rather than of *relationships.* There was nothing in their "relationship" to account for the lack of commitment, the flinging away, for the simple reason that to her, entirely unconsciously, their times and work together did not add up to "relationship" at all; no matter how intense or frequent, they remained episodes.

The difference between episode and relationship is profound. Relationships come in all shapes and sizes, as we all know. They may be formal or intimate, intense or casual, personal or impersonal, long or short. What underlies them all, though, is the sense of connectedness brought about when the people in them invest some parts of themselves in each other, in whatever way is appropriate to the nature of the relationship. What I am calling an "episode" may on the surface seem like a relationship—as it certainly did in the case I am describing here—but for the episodic person it lacks that essential bit of self-investment that in turn gives a relationship its appropriate degree of continuity and connectedness. The episode produces that "there but not there" feeling in an interaction, so often recognized in hindsight, once the shattered hopes and decimated plans have been cleared away.

All of us, of course, experience and use *both* kinds of

interaction all the time, depending on the circumstance. My buying some new clothing from a sales clerk I may or may not see again and in whose life I have no investment, nor he in mine, is properly an episode. My critiquing a theological student's work in class is part of a relationship, even though it will be of relatively brief and circumscribed duration, perhaps even less extensive in time than with the sales clerk. The difference lies in the exchange of self-investment. The same distinction applies to other kinds of experience besides personal interaction. I would say, for instance, that my going to a new city for a brief time of work or pleasure is an episode, while returning to a village I love on the coast of Northern Ireland where I find frequent restoration is more like a relationship—with the place or experience itself, if you please.

What my client sadly had to conclude about his friend was that she moves through life from one episode to another, and only rarely if at all ventures into relationships —with people, events, experiences, or places. The episodes may be quite intense, intimate, exciting, professionally competent, and "real," but when they are over they are over; no interconnecting investment links them together. Their friendship was a series of such episodes which never made it into what you could call a relationship. That was the underlying reason for the comings and goings that had been utterly baffling so long as he was assuming that what he was dealing with was a relationship, but which became clear and predictable once he saw the whole pattern as episodic.

That vignette, like the one involving my children, shows this: the real purpose of marriage vows is to express the partners' commitment to be in a relationship with each other rather than to live out a string of episodes, no matter how tightly interwoven and relationship-like they seem to be. And here I have to quibble a bit with our language, even as I myself have been using it: *vow and promise are not the same.* A promise is a guarantee of results, the sort of thing one will and can make about an episode, because it is circumscribed and within one's immediate experience and control. A vow is something very different; it is more a warranty of relationship, with all the uncertainty and ambiguity that entails, *except* that because it is a relationship there is vouchsafed some commitment and continuity to what unknown state will follow next. The vow grows in an atmosphere of perfectly awful ambiguity; the promise is safely sealed in predictability. The marriage vow is sign, seal, and vehicle of self-investment. It is not a "promise" that *even could* be kept on the same order of promising to do this or that; it is a commitment to work in relationship.

Obviously, then, a vow is a more pervasive, far-reaching kind of thing than a promise is. A vow is a person's pledge to invest him- or herself in a certain relationship, while promises have to do with more specific, concrete behaviors that may very well go on *within* the relationship the vow establishes. There is still more to the difference, however, and here I believe is the real value of the distinction we have been trying to make. The consequence of breaking a promise is appropriately some form of "punishment" or reparation. When my teenager promises to be in by eleven and does not appear until one in the morning, the consequence may be that he is grounded for the next week. When I promise to send a friend a book next week and forget to do it, I will be embarrassed and have to apologize and perhaps have to make a special trip to get the package into the mail. The more significant the promise and the more dire the consequences of breaking it, the more severe the reparation, as we all basically know when we come to think about it.

Vows are not "broken" in quite the same way, because the underlying meaning and "logic," if you please, of the vow is quite different. Since a vow is a pledge of investment of a certain kind and is therefore a pervasive commitment of a major part of one's whole life-style, no particular, finite event makes or breaks it. When we reach a point, however, where the investment the vow signifies is more absent than present, *then the relationship is in fact over.*[1] An oath of office, for instance, is a vow, and when the officeholder is no longer able or willing to arrange his or her life in such a way as to make good on the investment-pledge the vow represents, the appropriate consequence (either voluntarily or by outside force) is not punishment or reparation *but rather resignation of or removal from the office.* A friend of mine is a former Navy chaplain who discovered over the years that his beliefs about military service, his religious commitment, and his sense of public service had grown increasingly to conflict with his vows as a military officer. He was in many ways a model officer and chaplain and in fact was already clearly marked for rapid advancement in the leadership ranks. There was no question of breaking any promises and hence no consequence of punishment, but when he finally acknowledged that his investment in the relationship with the Navy had run out, he resigned because he could no longer consistently live out his vow. It was in fact the only honest and honorable thing to do, wrenching a decision though it was.

I would argue that the same basic understanding and logic should and does apply to marriage vows: it is not so much that divorce "breaks the vow" as that when the vow cannot be honestly and consistently sustained, the rela-

[1] Margaret A. Farley, *Personal Commitments: Beginning, Changing, Keeping* (San Francisco: Harper & Row Publishers, 1986) makes nearly the same point, pp. 85–109. Farley argues that the obligation to keep commitments is never absolute, but changes when those commitments become impossible. When a relationship has become impossible therefore the vow that established it is, in effect, set aside, much as it would be by the "impossible" condition created by death. See also Lewis B. Smedes, *Caring and Commitment: Learning to Live the Love We Promise* (San Francisco: Harper & Row Publishers, 1988).

tionship either should be or already has ended. The worry
that divorcing people have about their moral or spiritual
culpability in "breaking their vows" is in this sense exactly backward: it is rather precisely *because* the vow cannot any longer be lived out that the relationship it pledged
is over—and probably should be openly acknowledged.
Here then is a paradox which I have found comes in its
own strange way as a relief to many divorcing people:
*staying in a marriage when one no longer believes in or can live
out the marital vow is a greater and more hypocritical violation
of what that "vow" means than ending the marriage and acknowledging that one has failed.*

I seriously propose therefore that we stop using the language of "breaking the vows" of marriage, simply because
that kind of talk is inconsistent with the basic meaning of
what a vow is to begin with. We should speak of "broken
promises" when that is the case with specific acts, but of
"failed vows" when it comes to the basic marital commitment. The difference is crucial to this painful and often
foggy part of the spiritual journey of divorce.

I believe it is a heartbreak not to be able to live out the
content of those vows; but from what I have seen I would
have to say it can be an even greater and more widely
destructive heartbreak for people in miserable marriages
to subordinate the rest of their lives to the *sheer act of promising* because they have misunderstood the nature of the
vows they have taken. That is almost as though we were
trying to cover up the fallibility and sinfulness of the human condition and lay some claim to perfection by hanging on to the *act*, while the *relationship* that act committed
us to trying to create has clearly failed. To acknowledge
one's failure, to "repent" in traditional religious terms, is
to open oneself to the hope of renewal and forgiveness.
But to hang on to a ritual act as though it were magically
efficacious entirely apart from the human realities of a
failed relationship strikes me on spiritual grounds as a

form of the highest arrogance, a denial of the very need for restoration that every religious tradition I know of claims must be confessed before one's spiritual journey can be resumed. To my long-distance friend I had written, "All I want to say is that I *know* it is tragic the vows did not hold, but I also know, somehow, that the God before whom they were made is not limited to the finite grasping after surety that the language of my—or anyone's—promises represents."

Please do not think there is anything cavalier intended by this distinction between vow and promise. While I do not notice married people thinking or working much with their marriage vows, I do not believe for a minute that at the time they did not take them seriously. I have performed lots of weddings and presided over lots of failed marriages, but have hardly ever encountered a couple who said their vows cynically, facetiously, or even casually, no matter what their level of religious awareness was. In plain fact, a marriage is a special form of "contract," even in the legal sense, and every contract of whatever kind has some orderly provision for being set aside when it can no longer be performed on. No one would say that that means people routinely enter into contracts with their fingers crossed and their eyes on the loopholes. No, people enter contracts because they *intend* to perform on them in order to receive certain clearly identified advantages in return. In the anger of divorce one spouse will fairly often hurl an accusation at the other along the lines of, "What happened to those promises you made? How come you don't take them seriously?" No amount of protest that part of the present pain is that we *do* take them seriously but are caught in an unsolvable dilemma is likely to still the unspoken charge: you are a cynical, self-serving cad who didn't mean a word of what you said and headed for the door the moment hardship entered the picture. To be sure, there are relationships built on nothing but sand, at best, in which the kind and degree of commitment contains so little sense of vow that the slightest demand sends them reeling. They are "episodic" in the sense I described earlier. But even though at times I am not much of either an optimist or a romantic, I do not believe that those fairweather liaisons very often result in marriage. Particularly in this country, and particularly among spiritually oriented people marriage has not been a casual affair. We marry a lot, but we do not do so lightly.

All this is by way of saying that when divorce occurs I believe we can safely assume that some part of the pain—perhaps hidden from the awareness of the people involved—has to do with our guilt and despair over breaking vows once made in sincerity and love. Strangely enough, it is an aspect of the divorcing process that is seldom talked or written about, perhaps for the simple reason that it is hard to know what to say.

The failed marriage vow is not, after all, foreign to what most of us experience every day. It mirrors the condition of human brokenness under which we all live all the time. None of us likes it or freely chooses it. In the language of the Judaeo-Christian tradition, such vows are sometimes called "covenants," reminiscent of the covenant between a transcendent God and the people of God's creation. What we sometimes forget, though, is what both Old and New Testaments of the Bible say repeatedly, that no human attempt to duplicate the faithfulness of God's covenant has ever succeeded. If the story stopped there, we would have a spiritual journey ending in despair. The biblical story, however, goes on to say that this transcendent God redeems our brokenness not by curing it or setting it aside, thus violating our freedom, but rather by joining it in God's own brokenness. Whether it happens at Moab's field or on Golgotha, the point is the same: the pain of the broken vow is gathered up and transformed by that peculiar unbreaking brokenness of the very Creator. There is no magic here, and no eternal legislature sitting in solemn, judgmental assembly. There is instead a weeping, and holding, and binding up again, for violator and violated alike. "Someday" has come.

What, then, does the marriage vow do? It places us in a contract to build a relationship, and curiously enough sometimes that contract is fulfilled even when marriage ends, in storm and darkness, as we realize that we did as best we could what we promised to do. The theology of the marriage vow calls us to work toward creating a special relationship. It is a promise to *work*, not to succeed, because promising success is not something within the power of human beings to do. In the meantime, as a divorcing person I will have to take responsibility for all those ways in which I did not work hard enough, and perhaps ask forgiveness for them. But while I am on the subject, perhaps I will be able to remind myself that, despite what the language may have said, I promised to work toward reaching a goal. I did not, *could not*, promise the goal itself, because it was never in my power to do so. And what I may very well have forgotten is that the God in whose name and presence I took those vows has a much longer experience than I in dealing with failure.

You may have noticed something of a gap in this whole discussion. What about the basic question, "But isn't it *wrong* to break a promise or fail in a vow, whatever you choose to call it?" I wish that were a simple question, but it is not. To the whole subject of the "wrongness" of divorce we turn in the following chapter.

FIVE

Divorce Is Not a Sin

TO MY MIND there is hardly anything more damning than being forgiven for something you did not do. It is hard enough sometimes to let myself feel forgiveness when I know I have done wrong, but when I cannot connect with anything either my feelings or my conscience identify as wrong or "sinful," the experience is infinitely worse. If it happens often enough I may come to feel that as surely as where there is smoke there is fire, with so many people so vocally forgiving me I must have done *something* wrong even if I cannot figure out what it is. Undeserved guilt gets added to unnecessary confusion, as though there were not already quite enough of both in even the smoothest divorce experience. Something like that happens to divorcing people all the time, especially if they are actively religious, because of the best intentions of the church, spiritual leaders, and the lay public. I believe it is time to call a halt to it, which is the purpose of this chapter.

Most say that both religion's and the culture's attitude toward divorce today is more accepting and tolerant than it has ever been. Divorcing people do not carry the moral stigmata they used to, even as little as a generation ago, and while there is still a lot of misunderstanding and discrimination around, there also seems to be a lot more openness. Even in the Roman Catholic Church it is increasingly common (though still officially forbidden) for bishops and priests to permit divorced and remarried people to receive communion, something unheard of until recently. So far as the church is concerned, divorcing people are welcomed, not shunned, as they used to be. Despite all that, however, when people divorce they often also sever their religious ties. That ought to strike us as odd, just when things *seem* to be more accepting. Appearances, however, are not always reliable.

I have listened to a lot of ministers, lay people, and academic theologians talk about divorce, and if there is a standard, enlightened, "mainline" religious position on divorce these days I think it would run something like this:

> God intended for marriages to last, but because we are inherently sinful creatures, divorce sometimes happens anyway. Rather than condemning divorce or the divorcing, however, we should acknowledge that there is forgiveness for the sin of divorce just as there is for other sins, and so look pastorally on divorce as the painful, violating experience it is.

There are variations, of course, but that seems to me more or less the bottom line of current thinking and attitudes about the spiritual, religious dimension of divorce. On the surface it seems to be a humane, accepting perspective for which divorcing people might be expected to be grateful, especially compared to the old days.

Frankly, I do not believe it, and at the risk of being ungrateful, biting the hand that feeds me, and looking a gift horse in the mouth all at once, I want to draw the map from a different perspective that will serve us far better for the spiritual journey of divorce. Even on traditional theological grounds there are at least three things seriously wrong with that "enlightened" position: the assumptions (1) that divorce is a sin, (2) that it is necessarily a painful, shattering experience, and (3) that it is contrary to what God "wants" for people. Each of those assumptions contains something that is *almost* true—but not quite —and as a result they are misleading at best and falsely accusing at worst. Divorcing people who take the spiritual dimension of their experience seriously have a right to clearer theological thinking about it than has been commonly done, even by clergy and religious people whose own attitudes toward divorce are the very soul of love and acceptance.

DIVORCE IS NOT A SIN

The most egregious mistake we make is the almost casual assumption that *of course divorce is a sin*. We quickly follow that up with an assurance that it is an eminently *forgivable* sin, and pledge a noncondemning understanding and forgiveness to divorcing people. But on what grounds do we label divorce as sinful, wrong, a transgression in the first place? What warrants our even placing something as complex as a marital relationship and its ending in the particular theological category of "sin"?

Let us be clear that not everything we feel bad or angry or even sorry about is a sin (just as, frankly, there are some things that various segments of organized religion call "sin" which most other perfectly decent and moral people do not and should not care two hoots about). What the conventional wisdom overlooks is that divorce is a complex of behaviors and experiences, *some* of which may very well be sinful, but which is far too widely variable and complicated an experience to crowd under the umbrella of that single theological concept. If I am something of a moral traditionalist (which I am) I would say that adultery is a sin, as well as spouse or child beating, stealing the family bank account, lying, failing to pay agreed-on child support, or any of a whole list of things that *may* be part of the divorce picture. But again, they may not be.

The point is that labeling the whole complex of divorce as sinful casts too wide a net, and inescapably puts us in the position of being forgiven for something we did not do. Here, for instance, is a wife who has finally ended a stultifying marriage to an immature, unloving, and uncommitted husband who treated her as a sexual object and their children as trinkets of achievement. What does she hear when we say, no matter how "forgivingly," that her divorce is sinful? Or here is a couple who, after years of the most earnest and responsible effort, have acknowledged that they are poisoning each other's growth and fulfillment. With as much mutual goodwill as they can muster they face the fact that they are hurting each other more and more and have mortgaged emotional energy that might otherwise go outward to other people, their work, or their children. Perhaps one might say it would be sinful to continue such a marriage, but ending it simply does not fit that category: it is too complex for such a neat judgment. Or here again is a woman with a year-old child whose husband left her abruptly after the birth for the woman with whom he was having an affair at the time. What sense does it make to say *she* is forgiven for the "sin" of divorce?

I have never seen anyone just walk away from a marriage without making any attempt to figure out what went wrong. One of the hardest things for divorcing people to do is to sort out the complicated strands of their failed marriages, to try to come to some realistic sense of who is responsible for what—not blamable, mind you, but responsible, with a yawning difference in between. Each partner may at one time or another have been in the roles of victim and victimizer, rejecter and rejected, aggressor and target, manipulator and manipulated, passive and active, dominant and submissive, and on and on through a lengthy checklist of the ingredients of any marital relationship. For religious people it will be possible, even necessary, to add to that list the categories sinner and sinned against. Deciding when, under what circumstance, and perhaps why I carried first one role and then another is part of the hard work of coming to understand my divorce, partly so that I do not keep repeating negative behavior and partly so I can find something reasonably commendable about myself to hang on to when my self-esteem lies in tatters all about me. If I am concerned about the spiritual, value-laden dimension of the experience, I am also going to ask what I did wrong that needs my sorrow, my repentance, that needs forgiveness.

This accounting and responsibility-taking process, which seems so necessary for a healthy resolution to divorce, gets thoroughly muddled and confused by almost any sweeping, categorical judgments that fail to recognize the complexity of the experience. Saying that divorce is in and of itself sinful is just as unhelpful a statement as saying that one partner or the other is entirely at fault for the rift—something which is nearly never the case, no matter what things look like on the surface. The net effect, ironically and sadly, is to make it harder rather than easier to accept responsibility for our behavior in specific terms. It is rather like the person who makes the blanket self-judgment, "I'm no damned good" and thus lets himself or herself neatly off the hook of needing to determine precisely how and where repentance or improvement is needed. Or as a student of mine put it so beautifully, calling divorce a sin may cost us an opportunity of grace. In the process, by speaking so generally of the sin of divorce we may dodge the issue of *real* sinfulness and the need for repentance.

I remember a woman in process of divorce, for instance, who for months spoke not at all of her religious values until one counseling session when her level of guilt, real or imagined, got to the swamping point. Then it came out that whereas she had previously been a faithful church-goer, she had not darkened the door of her church since she and her husband separated. She held an exaggerated, blanketlike opinion of her own responsibility for the failed marriage, and considered herself unworthy of entering the church—not an uncommon view in such circumstances. I wondered out loud whether the church wasn't in business precisely for sinful people in need of restoration, and she quickly saw the religious Catch-22 she had constructed for herself: if she thought her "sinful" status made her unacceptable to the church, she was cutting herself off from the forgiveness and support the church offers sinners.

The more subtle underlying point, however, was that she had been unable to carry out a realistic sorting-through examination of her behavior in the marriage to find out just what particular things she might appropriately need forgiveness for. Part of the responsibility for that paralysis has to lie with this seemingly enlightened but actually rather insidious assumption about divorce—the whole thing—as "sin." I believe it is past time therefore to make this crucial distinction on theological as well as personal and spiritual grounds: certain behavior to be found in divorcing situations may indeed be "sinful" in its own right and call for repentance and forgiveness in whatever way one's religious tradition mandates, *but divorce itself is not a sin, neither as a complex of behaviors nor as the outcome of the process of getting unmarried.*

Some would say that such a position would surely be completely unacceptable to Roman Catholics if they wanted to be consistent with their theological belief structure. That is just not true. In a thoroughly ironic way, which large numbers of Catholic lay people do not realize, Roman Catholic teaching is the most liberal of all on the "sinful" designation of divorce. In Catholic sacramental theology *divorce is not possible.* Even civil divorces are not recognized by the Catholic Church, a fact which, of course, introduces another whole set of problems and issues for its divorcing members. But within the tightly argued theology that lies behind their position, the logic is unassailable: of course, divorce is not a sin, because marriages are inescapably permanent (except when annulled by the Church) and divorce therefore cannot, by definition, exist. It is simply not true, for instance, that divorced people are forbidden Holy Communion or any of the other sacraments or services of the Church. There are plenty of ways to be a sinful Catholic, but getting divorced will in and of itself not do the trick. (In case things seem too easy, I also have to point out that on the basis of this same logic, *remarriage* for a Catholic *is* a sin because it amounts to bigamy and adultery. When Roman priests refuse to conduct marriage ceremonies when either of the partners has been divorced, it is not because the divorce is seen as sinful, but because to perform the marriage would then bring about a sinful state of affairs. Protestants, in general, and I myself do not hold that theological position on either count, but I thought it important—and a bit refreshing in an ironic sense—to remind Catholic readers that *their* worries about the "sinfulness" of divorce lie elsewhere!

DIVORCE IS NOT ALL AGONY

Here I am walking a fine line. I certainly do not want to say anything to feed our already all-too-easy denial of the painfulness of the divorcing process. At the same time, I believe the second thing wrong with our conventional religious wisdom about divorce is the handwringing assumption it makes that divorce is inevitably and completely an excruciatingly painful, shattering experience. Sometimes it is, but sometimes it is not. My worry here is that people holding religious and spiritual values will feel forbidden to acknowledge the positive aspects of their experience, because we are, in effect, telling them how sorry we are for all the misery they are going through.

Denial is the great enemy of recovery from divorce. It is denial of the painfulness of what is happening that keeps people emotionally bonded long after a divorce decree is final. It is denial that keeps grief alive long after it should have been resolved. It is denial that keeps people from being able to enter into new, creative relationships. It is denial, mediated through a variety of other things such as fuzzy personal boundaries or dishonesty about real feelings, that injures children in divorce, far more than the divorce itself. What we do not always manage to include in the list, however, is acknowledgment that *denial of the positive, growth-ful aspects of divorce is just as hurtful as denial of the pain.* And the religious value that finds nothing to celebrate in divorce contributes unwittingly to that denial, even in its very pastoral supportiveness.

When I first was separated I was "ministered to," as clergy are apt to put it, by a long line of friends who

shared my sorrow, wept either with or for me, and generally did a marvelous job of being sympathetic and supportive. But out of all that holding I remember two en-
counters, in particular, as being especially meaningful.
One was with a friend who himself had gone through far
more hell in his marriage and divorce than I ever would,
and who when he first heard that I, too, was joining the
ranks of the divorcing, promptly came to my office and
with deep, sincere feeling congratulated me on cutting the
Gordian knot. I was so relieved I nearly cried: finally
somebody was, in effect, able to give me some permission
to feel good about the clearly positive aspects of what was
going on. The other encounter, less pleasant I fear, was
with a clergyman who came to pay a pastoral visit to me.
After a long time talking about nothing in particular he
finally got around to asking me "how I was doing." Well, I
replied, of course, there was a lot of difficulty, but on the
whole I had not felt better in years—whereupon he got up
and left after one more strained sentence!

Now to be sure, *any* loss experience shakes one's personal equilibrium and in that sense violates the stability of
a once integrated system. Even welcome losses (the departure of a despised supervisor, leaving a hated old house for
a carefully chosen new one, or trading in your rusted-out
Belchfire V-8) have that effect, and depending on how you
would define the word, you could call the result "painful."
I would go on to affirm that there are most likely no divorces in which some element of sadness does not enter in.
Obviously there is the inescapable unhappiness of admit-
ting that what we once thought would work has not. My
point is that we have, if anything, these days a surfeit of
empathetic concern for the pain of divorce but not enough
realistic affirmation of the joy divorce also sometimes
brings.

I sometimes ask counseling clients to make a list of the
positive things they are experiencing as a result of divorc-

ing. Often the assignment is greeted as either impossible or cruelly inappropriate—the conventional religious wisdom at work, whether people think they are religious or not. With enough perseverance, however, the lists begin to grow. I no longer have to pretend affection I don't feel. I have more "available" time for the kids. I am not fighting and angry so much. I never realized sex could be so fun and loving. I have a sense of vocation again. I'm not drinking as much. Those chronic headaches have gone away. My old hobbies are fun again. I'm making new friends of both sexes. I don't have to lie to friends and family about my marriage. I've learned some new skills and interests. I'm able to let people nurture me now. I'm loving a living space of my own. I have a better sense of self now. I'm not so tired at the end of every day. And so on it will go, different for everyone.

I may ask people whether it does not seem appropriate to be *thankful* for those things, in whatever religious framework is meaningful for them. I may need to remind them that mixed feelings about nearly everything are the emotional norm, not an aberration, and that feeling good about parts of their divorcing experience neither edges out nor is canceled by feeling pretty awful about other parts. Just as in grieving for the death of a loved one the hardest time may be allowing oneself to begin feeling good again, lest it seem a betrayal of the lost one's memory, so, too, in divorce feeling good about the joyful aspects may be made more difficult by the notion that one *ought* to be pretty unrelievedly gloomy about the whole thing—though of course one is "forgiven" in the end!

"WHOM GOD HATH JOINED TOGETHER . . ."

Though it is probably not apparent yet, we have now stumbled onto an important distinction between theological interpretation and actual human experience. It can be argued that people's experience of something as positive and joyful is no warrant for giving it a clean theological bill of health. Or to put it more bluntly, just because I may be feeling generally good about my divorce may not for a minute mean that *God* thinks it is such a hot idea. Here is the assumption made, especially in organized religion, that no matter how necessary and forgivable and even positive divorce may be, it is nevertheless not what God intended as the fate of marriage. Once again, we are in the mode of being forgiven for something that would not have happened if things had gone according to plan—God's plan in this version. It may not matter much how your own religious or theological formulation phrases the basic idea. Some people will speak in traditional Judaeo-Christian terms of God's will and intention, while others will want to speak more generally of a cosmic harmony and congruence in terms of which human action and experience are assessed. Whatever the imagery used to express it, however, the basic idea is that marriage, once begun, is not supposed to be stopped, and that since divorce is not what God or nature intended, it is inescapably a spiritual and theological negative, no matter what one may *feel* about it.

I have no doubt that at least in some sense all that is true, as we will be exploring in more critical detail in Chapters Six and Seven. Religious people especially, however, have a way of talking rather fast and loose about what "God intends," and that I am frankly uncomfortable with, if not suspicious of. I have done it myself often enough and not always with the carefulness I am trying to campaign for here. Often, however, I have the rather distinct impression that what we are talking about when we speak of cosmic intent is what *we would prefer*, perhaps on the most incontrovertible moral, psychological, or social grounds. On theological grounds, however, any such assertion is complicated, if not downright dubious, for three main reasons, two of which I want to talk about here and the third of which begins the next chapter.

One reason is that such language of desire, intentionality, or will is always human talk, the sort of things we will say about how *we* behave. In technical terms, such talk puts the deity into a human mold, anthropomorphizes God. All religions do it to some degree or another, and the Judaeo-Christian tradition has always spoken of God in such human terms. Nothing could be more natural, since the only language we have is human, after all, and the basic foundation plank of Judaeo-Christian theology is that the infinite God of the universe has a particular love and regard for the human beings that same God created. At the same time, it has always been one of the jobs of theology to serve as a watchdog on the way we speak of God, so that even though human imagery is unavoidable, we remain self-conscious and self-critical about it, always mindful that our human terms can never fully describe or capture what is infinite and eternal. We try to remain aware, in other words, that such talk about God is always metaphorical, always filtered through the lens of human perception and imagery.

Here again we make the mistake of talking about divorce as though it were a single, well-defined "thing" when in fact it is a widely diverse complex of behaviors. About *some of those behaviors* I believe we can on solid theological grounds make some "God intends" statements, based in part in the Judaeo-Christian framework on what the Bible has to say. To extend those judgments to divorce as a total, diverse phenomenon, however, defies logic. I am not uncomfortable, for instance, with saying that victimizing other people for our own ends is contrary to God's intention, and there is certainly a lot of victimizing that goes on in both divorces and marriages. It is painful, psychologically destructive, and immoral; but it would be irresponsible to spread our judgment about victimizing over the whole subject of divorce, even though we do so routinely in religious circles. The same would be true about a long list of items that *may* be involved in a divorce: lying, cruelty, adultery, selfishness, self-deception, and all the rest.

The second reason for being very cautious with "God intends" statements about divorce is that any such statements are at least as much statements about the culture from which they spring as they are about God. This is an extension to a cultural level of the language reservation just discussed. So far as we know, every culture in human history, and very likely in prehistory as well, based on what evidence we have, has made provision for stabilizing and regularizing itself in what we would call "marriages" of one shape and hue or another. Marriage always carries with it certain expectations, rituals, and even laws, varying with its culture. We also know, however, that every culture has at the same time made some provision for ending those marriages in a regular, reliable way under at least certain circumstances. Simply stated: *both* marriage and divorce are built into human culture right at the bedrock. How a culture or a society felt about divorce has always depended upon how it valued marriage. Where the survival of the society virtually required that marriages be stable, divorce was made very difficult. Where the society expanded into sufficient complexity that the marital unit itself was not the only or even the essential factor in its survival, divorce was easier (and more common). Granted, this is oversimplifying the picture rather considerably, but the basic point is accurate.

Any religion represents a byplay between what its people hold to be the revelation of ultimate truth from God and the cultural needs and wishes of its believers. What "God intends" for marriage is, then, at least in part a culturally conditioned statement, a perfectly appropriate way for a people to express how significant are its most paramount, ultimate values. Whether that can be taken as equivalent to a revelation of transcendent purpose is, however, another matter. Of course I, like most people, hope that marriages last. But if that hope, widely shared in the culture, gets expressed as a statement of God's own intent and purpose, it takes on a compelling, even judging dimension that is a new ingredient. To fall short now is not to fall short of what you and I and everybody else wants—admittedly—but to fall short of the intent of God, and that puts the whole matter into a moral framework it did not have before.

I will say a good deal more about this point in the next two chapters on the primary source of information about what "God intends" for both Christians and Jews, the Bible itself. My primary aim here is, essentially, to get us to clean up our language both in and out of church and temple when we talk globally about the spiritual characteristics of divorce. To the divorcing person who is wearing the equivalent of a scarlet letter *D* around his or her neck, I have to say: "Take it off. Search through your own behavior with as much thoroughness and professional help, both psychological and religious, as you need and come to terms with the list of things you have done that are genuinely culpable in the moral or spiritual value system to which you adhere. To *those* you may freely give the label "sinful" and proceed accordingly. But to "divorce" itself, that word does not apply, no matter what else we may say about it.

Since a good many otherwise clearheaded clergypersons are "guilty" of the linguistic carelessness I have taken to task in this chapter, perhaps the following endnote is in order. During the years of preparing this book I have had numerous occasions to discuss its ideas, and this one in particular, with a wide variety of clergy. With the exception of a few members of what I would have to identify as the fundamentalist right end of the theological spectrum, whose internal consistency I frankly believe is dubious, virtually every such minister hearing my challenge to his or her most "liberal" theological opinion about divorce has first blinked, more or less scratched his or her head, and then said something like, "Yeah, now that I think of it, that's *right!*" I am not intending to insert my own opinion poll here in support of my position. I am rather trying to note (and forewarn you) that, on the basis of some first-hand evidence, the trouble with the "mainline enlightened" theological position on divorce is that it has just not thought through the implications of what it says. When it does so, it typically shifts in the direction I have been arguing.

A clergy friend of mine who views matters much as I do had preached a sermon on divorce to his congregation shortly before we talked about the contents of this chapter. In the sermon he had taken a movingly pastoral and accepting position on the "sinfulness" of divorce, but the old categorization was nevertheless there. At least one couple in the throes of divorce had walked out of the worship service. After we had talked it through, he preached a second sermon on divorce making the distinctions I have argued for here. He reported that the clarity and relief it brought to his hearers was markedly evident. The point I am making is that even the most theologically well-trained, tolerant, and pastorally sensitive ministers can fall into this particular language trap. We ministers are learning as we go just as you as a divorcing person are. Don't give up on us, but don't let us off the hook either!

SIX

What the Bible Doesn't Say About Divorce

IT IS INTRIGUING to me how, when it comes to divorce, even people who are not particularly religious or consumers of the Bible seem to have a concern for what it has to say about their predicament. People who otherwise would not give a second thought to "what the Bible says" about anything seem to feel differently when divorce is the issue. Even if you have not opened a Bible in years (or ever), the chances are good that somewhere in your divorce experience someone, if not yourself, is going to bring the whole question of "what the Bible says" into the picture, perhaps for no other reason than that popular religious culture often seems so preoccupied by it. The question I want to pose (and try to answer) in this and the following chapter therefore is one I have heard in many different ways from divorcing people, ranging across the spectrum from highly religious to completely secular. Whatever form one's concern with the broadly spiritual dimension of divorce takes, however, the question is never asked purely as a matter of curiosity; someone's anguish and need always show: *"Does the Bible have a clear word for us about divorce?"* That is what we want to find out.

This chapter talks about how one reads the Bible and applies it to one's life in the first place, and then summarizes what it does—and perhaps more important, does *not* —say about divorce. Rather than make one doubly long chapter, I have taken yet another one to talk in more specific detail about the three most significant texts in the Bible about divorce, what we sometimes call the "hard sayings," the ones that give ordinary readers (and biblical scholars, too!) the most difficulty on this already difficult subject. At the end of the next chapter we will see more specifically what I believe is the Bible's genuinely clear "word" about divorce.

A biblical scholar once commented that if you took a dozen or so of the very best of his colleagues and set them the task of describing clearly what the Bible says about divorce, you would get a dozen or so wildly different results—all equally informed and accurate! That is not actually such an "iffy" proposition, as the shelves of any good theological library will attest. The best and most faithful students of the Bible differ about what the book means on the subject. Whether those writers are talking on the highly technical level of the precise meaning of Hebrew and Greek texts, on what you might call the "applied theological" level of the meaning and intent of what is written, or on the personal and spiritual level of what impact the Bible might have on someone who turns to it for clarification, guidance, or comfort, the picture is essentially the same: there are commonly identified themes and ideas and unanswered questions, but on some aspects of the subject there is little agreement.

It does not take long to find out why things are so confused and confusing: when we speak of "the Bible," or rather loosely talk about "what the Bible says," we risk rolling into one too-easy ball of language a number of separate and important things. Some are obvious, but some are not. For instance, most everybody would quickly realize that "the Bible" includes (for Christians) both Old and New Testaments, and that the whole of those writings covers a time span of several thousand years and a cultural spectrum at least as great and diverse as one finds in Western civilization *since* the close of the New Testament's pages. It would be strange indeed if a good deal of diversity, development, and downright contradiction did *not* occur in such a span. It may be less obvious to many people that even *within* what seem like reasonably self-contained parts of the Bible a similar variability occurs. Within the Old Testament, for instance, there is a considerable difference between Jewish law and understanding from the time of Moses, through the period of the later prophets, and into the "modern" period of Pharisaic Judaism around the time of Jesus. The same would be true, though in a more compressed time zone, of the New Testament between, say, the teachings of Jesus and the understanding of the apostle Paul.

There are other major differences to compound the matter beyond the actual biblical texts themselves, chief among them being the question of how people read, understand, and value the Bible. The Bible will "say" one thing to someone who approaches it with a more literal temper, and something very different to another kind of reader. A person who sees the Bible as the attempt of religious people to understand, interpret, and pass on what they experienced as the work of a transcendent God in their lives will hear something very different, perhaps, from the one who views the Bible as a definitive statement of God's cosmic laws for human behavior. In other words, added to the internal and intrinsic complexity of the Bible as a collection of documents is the equal and opposite complexity of the attitudes of its readers, what they bring to it and inescapably add to what we so oversimply refer to as its "meaning." The wonder is not that on a given subject there is confusion, but rather that, despite all this, the Bible still *does* manage to speak reliable words of insight, guidance, and hope to many different kinds of people in countless different situations.

The intent of all this is not to discourage you (and most assuredly not to discourage you from turning to the Bible for help and interpretation) but rather to put a large orange CAUTION sign over any approach you may happen to find to the topic of divorce in the Bible that makes it seem uncomplicated, pat, or dogmatic. Things are both far worse but also far better than that, as I hope we shall now see.

To come back to the question with which we began, I want to give a direct answer and describe what I am trying to get for us out of this chapter. "Does the Bible have a clear word for us about divorce?" No, frankly, it does not. For reasons I am going to spend some time with now, I believe it is time we declared a draw on that subject, in order that we can take a second step: *The Bible does not have a clear word about divorce, but it* does *have a clear word about something far more important: the restoration of broken human beings.* When we have understood the first, we will be ready to reach out for the second, and that is the real purpose of this chapter.

THE BIBLE'S UNCLEAR WORD ABOUT DIVORCE

One can only admire the skill and tenacity of biblical scholars in attempting to reconstruct something of what both ordinary and religious life must have been like in ancient times. Single Bible verses or even phrases are often the *only* evidence we have of this or that practice, belief, or ritual. That through scholars' researches and interpretations we have some sort of more or less whole picture of life in Bible times is, to my way of thinking, at least as inspired and miraculous a turn of events as is that sacred volume itself! Alongside such genuine appreciation, however, a caveat is needed: the actual textual evidence for much of what we "know" about how the biblical world operated is sometimes very slim indeed. That need not keep us from drawing conclusions and forming hypotheses; but it certainly ought at the same time to remind us that uttering the phrase "the Bible says" is often a very precarious business.

The subject of divorce in the Bible is a classic case of the need for just this sort of cautiousness. The basic reason for that is the nature of the Bible itself, which may come as a surprise to some people. The Bible is a collection of writings of great diversity held together by one common concern and theme: discerning and describing the work of the creator God of the universe in the lives of human beings who believe that they are this God's people. Those who, intending to be skeptically liberal, value the Bible as a great collection of poetry, moral teachings, ancient wisdom, guides for ethical living, or whatnot are mistaken in one fundamental way: while the Bible indeed contains all those things, it never intends to be *any* of them. It intends to be the story of the mighty acts of its God as experienced and reflected on in the lives of those with whom that God has dealt over the centuries. Now within that rather broad definition is room for much variety and disagreement about how the Bible is to be interpreted, what weight it has or should have in one's practical life or religious faith, and what the source of its authority should be taken to be.

The Bible being what it is therefore means that there are lots of things it is *not*. The Bible is almost never concerned, for instance, with the daily life and times, problems and opportunities, aches and joys, feelings and impressions of the people who inhabit its pages. I remember the late Paul Scherer, one of the great preachers and teachers of this century, and as passionately involved as any human being I knew in the lives of the people he served, often commenting how surprising it was that the Bible was hardly concerned at all about *what you and I feel*. The reason for that is that the dominant focus of its various writings, as I said before, is on the writers' religious, beyond-the-ordinary experience. It is easy to excuse the absence of so much everydayness by saying that lots of modern problems just did not exist in biblical times and so, of course, they would not be found talked about. Unfortunately, it won't wash. A great number of "modern" human issues *were indeed* alive and well in those days, and about them the Bible remains a silent book. Even then people got old and died, fell ill and were treated by the medicine of the day, wrote and read controversial literature, experienced social disruption and decay, came to the ends of their working lives, had their fortunes overturned by hostile governments and wars, fell in love and conducted courtships, raised children and educated them, practiced their trades and professions, developed urban cultures, built and managed economies through prosperity and depression, developed religions and religious conflicts, *and, in short, experienced all the species of human enterprise, conflict, brokenness, and victory we do today*. But on the details of virtually all of them the biblical authors scarcely say a word, simply because that was not the kind of writing they were trying to do. One could say with a minimum of argument, I think, that having tried to describe the work and will of the God they worshiped, the biblical authors left it up to us—then and now—to live all that out in the specifics of our days, applying and interpreting and refining for and by ourselves what they believed God had revealed about God's aims and purposes in creation.

So there are lots of things you will not find in the Bible. To illustrate the point, let me invite you to make a mental list of the things you are working most centrally with in your life this week. My own would include the following: deciding what to do about a possible job and geographical change, managing a strained budget, dealing with my children's educational needs and college planning, trying to determine how to be an effective parent amidst changing values between generations, writing a book, building a new relationship with a woman I love, cultivating a good working relationship with some difficult colleagues, trying to be responsible at long distance to parents who are growing older, and monitoring some important though not life-threatening personal health issues. There. It is not a dramatic or unusual list, probably not materially different from most of yours. I turn to my religious faith and to the biblical witness for guidance and support and community in dealing with all those things, *but there is not a specific word about any of them in the Bible.* It does no good to argue that biblical writers did not experience those things, because the plain truth is that both specifically and in cultural equivalents *they did.* It is just that the Bible is not that kind of book.

That is why I am saying in this chapter that the Bible does not have a clear word for us about divorce: as a subject it is largely just not there. To be specific, divorce is mentioned a total of fifteen times in the whole of the Bible, ten times in the Old Testament and five in the New. If, by extension, one wanted to add to the list a few places where things like marriage or adultery were talked about in context of ending marriages, you might eke out another half dozen occurrences. The longest of those "mentions" is seven verses. To be sure, those few verses have occasioned a lot of detailed scholarly writing—and perhaps even more careless pontificating. Our understanding of ancient Jewish and Christian religious practice is the richer for it, as is our theological sense of what it means to reach for and take into human experience what we believe to be the will of the transcendent God. Our understanding and spiritual or moral sense of divorce, however, is hardly touched.

Here is one of the two greatest stumbling blocks I have discovered for people who try to take the biblical witness seriously in thinking about their own (or others') divorcing: the *way* we handle the subject of divorce for ourselves is for the most part not addressed biblically. We tend to be concerned about whether divorce, in and of itself, is right or wrong; the biblical writers more typically approach divorce *in the context of* something else (women's rights, for instance, or the religious purity of Israel, to mention two occasions that produce *opposite* views of the rightness of divorce) which, in turn, determines how they view it. Or to put it differently, the biblical writers discuss *regulations for* divorce, but not the rightness or wrongness of divorce *itself.* Under certain conditions it is right and necessary, but under others it is not. We tend to be concerned about the impact of divorce on families and society and about what we could call the whole *relational* dimension of the experience; that is a level of thinking for the most part missing in the Bible. The closest it comes is in its concern for the rights of women and the purity of Israel's religion.

We tend to be concerned about our emotional responses to divorce and how the shattered personal lives of ourselves and our families can be reintegrated and gotten going again; the biblical writers, while certainly not inhumane or impersonal, simply do not think in that way, certainly on the subject of divorce.

Despite all the controversy and wrangling over details, it is surprisingly easy to summarize what the Bible does and does not actually say about divorce. The points of conflict tend to arise over how what it says can or should matter to us as twentieth century people. I believe it will be easiest to condense this material into a series of numerical items and discuss each briefly before we turn to a broader-gauged discussion of the Bible and divorce and then move to our concern in Chapter Seven, what sort of word the Bible *does* have to offer to those of us who are divorcing.

First, divorce is an assumed fact of life in the Bible. Every reference is to divorce as an already existing practice, under a variety of conditions. In other words, at no point in the Bible do we hear either Jewish or early Christian society take up the question, "Shall we permit divorce and if so under what guidelines?" On that basic question, it is silent. What the biblical world did is what every civilization known has done, provide structures and procedures for divorce so that some protection for innocent parties might be had and the chaos of unregulated marital anarchy avoided. The intention of divorce legislation is partly humane. In the early years of Israel's history, for instance, the penalty for a woman caught in adultery was for her and her lover to be executed. Allowing her husband to divorce her under those circumstances was an alternative that I imagine most of us would say is preferable. In short, the Bible does *not* say that divorce is forbidden. It does say that certain circumstances (such as adultery—or in later times, anything that displeases her husband!—on the woman's part) warrant divorce, while others do not.

Second, the Bible does not like *divorce (any more than anyone else I have ever heard of) even when it is allowed.* It does, particularly in the Old Testament, regulate certain aspects of the divorcing process in order to protect such things as the rights of women, the purity of Jewish religious practice, or the conduct of the priesthood. At the same time it spends exactly zero space talking about divorce as a social phenomenon with consequences for the culture, families, religious participation, values, the status or quality of marriage, or any other of the things we worry about in the modern world as significantly affected by failed marriages. Here is the place to make an important distinction, however: not liking something is not at all the same thing as saying it is morally or legally wrong.

Third, the Bible says that marriages are intended *to be permanent, but it does* not *say that they* in fact *are.*[1] That is, through divorce marriages can be ended in the eyes of both God and humankind. We will be coming back to this point in the next chapter when we talk about the famous "they shall become one flesh" verse of the Bible and what that means—and does not mean—about the inherent permanence of marriage.

Fourth, in the Old Testament divorce is categorized as "disciplinary" when the grounds are adultery of the wife or abuse (active or passive) on the part of the husband, or "treacherous" when the grounds are a man's wishing to divorce a wife in order to be with another woman. The former type of divorce is approved, while the latter is not, even though both are legally permitted.[2]

Fifth, divorce on grounds of mutual incompatibility, where

---

[1] William F. Luck, *Divorce and Remarriage: Recovering the Biblical View* (San Francisco: Harper & Row, Publishers, 1987) p. 25.

[2] Luck, pp. 69, 82. The terms "disciplinary" and "treacherous" are Luck's categorization.

one or both partners (in the absence of either abuse or adultery) agree to end the marriage for any of a variety of "modern" reasons is nowhere mentioned in the Bible, neither for approval nor condemnation.

This is the second of the two great stumbling blocks I mentioned regarding the Bible and divorce: one of the most common kinds of divorce situation experienced today is simply not "covered" by anything the Bible has to say about it. I am thinking particularly of the badly eroded marriage that in the quaint but highly descriptive language of the Episcopal church is in a state of "irretrievable breakdown," which its occupants choose to end in order to seek a better quality of life for themselves and/or their families. "Abuse" or adultery either is not present or if so is secondary to the main dynamics of a marriage we would say has "failed" socially, morally, psychologically, and (as we will see momentarily) *spiritually or theologically.* To be sure, in our grandparents' generation such marriages most likely would simply have been endured, and to find them now in the courts under the category, perhaps, of "no fault" divorce makes them look like a newer phenomenon than they in fact are. How extensive such marital failures were in ancient times is largely unknown. A case can be made that people did not so much think that way about marital relationships then, the idea of "love" *as the basis for marriage* being a more modern, late nineteenth-century European invention. Whatever was the case, that is not a category of divorce the Bible knows about, making it particularly hard for many people involved today to "hear" the Bible talking directly to them.

Sixth, in the New Testament Jesus is represented as saying three and only three things about divorce:

(a) he recognizes the Jewish law and practice on the subject, though, as in other of his teachings, he states a more extreme and demanding version of it;

(b) he condemns a man divorcing his wife on grounds *other than* "immorality" but is silent on the question of a woman divorcing her husband on grounds of mistreatment;[3] and

(c) he judges that other than in the divorces he excludes (female "immorality"), remarriage (though clearly possible under the law) makes the new partner of the formerly married adulterous.

We will be coming back to this "hard" line in the next chapter, but here is the place to resolve one frequently asked question: Is that what Jesus really meant in terms of the language he used and the reference he had in mind? The answer, I am afraid, is yes. Biblical scholars point out that the essentially single saying of Jesus on divorce is one of the most reliably free from later interpretation and augmentation of any in the New Testament. He was taking a hard line, without doubt. What that *means* to us today, in context of everything else Jesus was saying, is something else again, to which we will shortly turn; but to the question, "Does Jesus really come down so hard on divorce?" the answer is unambiguously affirmative.

Seventh, on only one occasion does a biblical writer refer to what God *thinks about divorce.* In one of the most often quoted (and least well explained) verses, Malachi 2:16, the Old Testament prophet is condemning Israelites who have

[3] Most scholars would say that in the biblical world a woman could not divorce her husband for any reason, or at best for only a few limited ones in the later Roman period; for the most part it was entirely a one-sided business, consistent with the dismal (by today's standards) position the Ancient Near Eastern world accorded women. Luck (pp. 26–36) attempts to make a case, however, that the Exodus 21 discussion of the rights of *concubines,* which include their right to leave their masters in the event of abuse or nonsupport, should also be understood to apply to wives. His logic is that if such rights were available to people in the relatively lower status of concubinage, they would surely also have been to wives. It is, frankly, a weak argument, not accepted by many scholars, largely because the complicated social structure of concubinage cannot be read as simply a diluted version of marriage.

abandoned the wives of their own race in order to marry foreign women. The purity of the nation is being threatened and the religious (though not "legal") sanction against "treacherous" divorce is being widely abused. The text reads, "So take heed to yourselves and let none be faithless to the wife of his youth. 'For I hate divorce says the Lord the God of Israel, and covering one's garment with violence, says the Lord of hosts.' "

Eighth, remarriage is permitted *throughout the entire Bible, though it is not* approved of *in certain cases of adultery or "treacherous divorce."* In the New Testament, for instance, the Apostle Paul speaks to the situation of a believer married to an unbeliever and permits divorce and remarriage.

Ninth, and finally, every mention of divorce in the Bible is "in passing," in the context of talking about something else, with divorce cited in reference to it as either a "for instance" or an application, or as an isolated brief statement. Divorce is not found anywhere in the Bible as a topic of sustained discussion in its own right; the longest text involving the subject is seven verses (Mt. 19:3–9).

This is not intended to be a chapter in biblical scholarship, but particularly among practicing Christians I have found the subject so shot through with misunderstanding and plain lack of information that I believe it will be helpful to identify and summarize *all* the explicit biblical references to divorce. There are only about fifteen such occurrences, though, of course, other passages having to do with marriage, adultery, mixed religion, and the like have an indirect bearing on the subject of divorce. If, however, a conscientious Bible reader wants to be able to identify and turn to all occurrences of the word "divorce" and its associated forms, here is a catalog:

Deuteronomy 22:19: If a man falsely accuses his wife of not being a virgin, he may not later divorce her.

Deuteronomy 22:29: If a man seduces an unbetrothed virgin and is found, he must marry her and cannot divorce her.

Deuteronomy 24:1-4: A man may not remarry his divorced wife after she has been remarried and divorced again from someone else.

Isaiah 50:1: Refers incidentally to a "bill of divorce."

Jeremiah 3:1,8: Uses an analogy of a divorced man remarrying former wife (cp. Deut. 24).

Malachi 2:16: Uses the "I hate divorce" analogy to decry Israel's faithlessness, condemning marriage to foreign women.

Leviticus 21:7,14: Priests are not allowed to marry divorced women. As we will see in Chapter Seven, this priestly standard becomes important for understanding the New Testament treatment of divorce.

Leviticus 22:13: A priest's divorced daughter may return home and eat his food.

Numbers 30:9: A man cannot nullify a divorced woman's vow or oath, as he can an undivorced woman's.

Ezekiel 44:22: Same as Lev. 21:7: priests cannot marry divorced women.

Matthew 1:19: Describes Joseph's intention to "divorce" his betrothed Mary for legal cause on the assumption that, being pregnant, she was no longer a virgin.

Matthew 5:31-32: Jesus says in the "Sermon on the Mount" that for a man to divorce his wife, except on ground of immorality, makes her an adulteress and that a man marrying a divorced woman commits adultery.

Matthew 19:3-9: In the longest passage on divorce in the Bible, Jesus replies to the Pharisees' test question regarding legality of divorce.

Mark 10:2-12: Essentially the same as the above.

Luke 16:18: Identical to Matthew 5:31.

I Corinthians 7:10-15: Paul addresses the question of divorcing an unbeliever, concluding it is permitted but not required.

Most people who are concerned about the biblical view, to begin with, gravitate to three passages in particular, and to a more focused and critical discussion of them the next chapter turns.

SEVEN

The "Hard Sayings" of the Bible About Divorce

AS I READ the biblical materials and scholarship and talk with divorcing people trying to find some spiritual bearings in the experience through the Bible, three particular concerns become most focal, each with a biblical text about divorce to back it up. After the previous chapter's general orientation to how the Bible handles the subject, I want to look more specifically at those three rough spots:

1. the saying that God "hates divorce";
2. the biblical picture of people entering marriage and becoming "one flesh," which may not be "sundered"; and

3. Jesus' apparent equation that divorce (and presumably remarriage) creates adultery and adulterers.

"GOD HATES DIVORCE" (MALACHI 2:16)

I was leading a discussion group of recently divorced people not long ago, and one deeply troubled woman whose husband had simply gotten tired of being married and left her (though the story was certainly more complicated than that) expressed her anguish over the biblical saying "God hates divorce." She had turned to the church for support and understanding, and being a member of this church-sponsored group was providing both those things. But it seemed something of a sham to her because of that verse etched on her mind: how could the church be so accepting when God hates divorce?

There are at least two things that such a person needs to hear, one about the text itself and a second about what it in fact says. The text is part of the prophecy of Malachi in the Old Testament and comes toward the end of what can only be described as a righteously indignant prophetic tirade against certain men of Israel who had without just cause abandoned their *Israelite* wives to marry women from *other* nations. The integrity of Israel's identity was clearly threatened by such a trend, and such "treacherous" divorce was clearly prohibited by Mosaic law. This text in no way attempts to set aside the divorce permitted under the law; it is really concerned with "national security," and is aimed specifically at the miscegenation that threatened it. Much more than that about either the situation or the prophet himself we do not know. But at the climax of his speech, as he is declaring what he believes to be the word of the Lord, comes the famous verse, "For I hate divorce, says the Lord God of Israel." (Mal. 2:16)

In and of itself that was a familiar form of prophetic

pronouncement. In the prophetic literature God is represented as "hating" all kinds of things that threaten the covenantal faithfulness of the people Israel. It should, of course, be kept in mind that the main thrust of the passage, its "topic" if you please, is not divorce at all but the tattered faithfulness of Israel to the covenant with its God. Malachi enumerates several ways in which Israel's faithlessness has been acted out; one of them is by taking foreign wives *and thereby failing to produce "Godly offspring" (Mal. 3:15)*, as would be the case with Israelite wives. That leads to this "hard saying" about divorce. Here, in other words, is one of those classic biblical occasions where divorce is used as a vehicle or "for instance" to point to the larger subject, in this case the faithfulness (or lack thereof) of Israel to God's covenant in general and the resulting threat to Israel's integrity and survival as a beleaguered nation.

What weight one gives that in terms of modern personal belief about divorce is, of course, a highly individual matter. What mostly concerns me about people's response to that text, exemplified by the woman I mentioned, is that they stop much too soon in hearing what it is saying. I am tempted to reply, with no facetiousness whatever, "God hates divorce? So do I. So do most people I know, and I would be badly disappointed if God somehow thought it was an inconsequential or benign thing to do." On theological grounds we would say, without hesitation, that God "hates" all kinds of things: suffering, injustice, hardness of heart, death, mistreatment of helpless people, sin of all kinds, and so on. In fact, the entire story of the people of the Bible is shot through with God's chosen servants doing things that God "hates" and God reestablishing a covenant of love and justice with them. In other words, God's "hating" something is not at all the end of the story but something closer to its beginning. With divorce specifically I seriously doubt that anyone who has been divorced considers remarrying without a conscious effort to make a better go of it the next time, without, so to speak, an effort at major change and what the Bible may call "repentance." And that, of course, is precisely the kind of response that Malachi (and most other biblical writers) are trying to elicit. Part, indeed, of my own sense of the spiritual journey divorce represents has to do with learning more about myself so that I do not make the same mistakes again, conduct a loving relationship as badly, interpret needs and signals of other people as erroneously, or misjudge as often the impact my own behavior was having on people close to me. God hates divorce? So do I. But as a result of it I have a better shot at being a more responsible partner and human being, and that seems to me the very thing God keeps trying to get me more involved with as what God wants from people who seek to live in a covenantal relationship.

The woman I referred to had made a serious mistake in her way of understanding the Bible: she had assumed that because God hates divorce she herself as a divorcing person was condemned and perhaps even cast out. If you take the Bible seriously, exactly the opposite conclusion presents itself: God's hatred *of the act* (never of the person) is a part of God's effort to love people and bring them back into relationship with their Lord. At the end of the day it is from my failure and my suffering and, when it is accurate to use the terms, my sinfulness and repentance that God mostly fashions the life-giving relationship promised to people of faith.

"THEY SHALL BE ONE FLESH" (GENESIS 2:24)

The words of Genesis, quoted by Jesus in Matthew 19, are a familiar part of many contemporary wedding ceremonies. ". . . A man shall leave his father and mother and be joined to his wife, and the two shall become one flesh. So they are no longer two but one. What therefore God has joined together, let no one put asunder" (Mt. 19:5–6). The words are familiar, but the question is what do they mean? Does the "one flesh" image constitute a biblical prohibition of divorce?

The answer is no. Far too many divorcing people are afraid that they mean something is created in marriage that *cannot* be undone (no matter what the civil law may say) and that to pretend or to act otherwise is an offense in the eyes of God or the church or general spiritual sensitivity. The "one flesh" image seems to suggest a merger of separate identities so that we are now speaking of a single corporate being, uniquely the result of marriage. While some interpretation may take such a position and build it into ecclesiastical doctrine, it is important to notice that the Bible itself seems to mean no such thing.

William Luck argues extensively, persuasively, and technically that the "one flesh" image in both Old and New Testaments refers basically to sexual union, in or out of marriage.[1] Linguistically, that is hard to argue with since the Bible uses the term to refer to physical unions both licit and illicit, with wives, concubines, and prostitutes alike. Not all are approved, needless to say, but all are considered examples of being "one flesh." Marriage just happens to be the proper context of the one-flesh relationship. Luck further argues that while in marriage the *intention* is that the relationship be permanent, it is a permanency of intention and commitment, not necessarily of fact, sad as that outcome may be. The Bible's view, argues Luck, does not hold the marital union to be a "mysteri-

---

[1] William F. Luck, *Divorce and Remarriage: Recovering the Biblical View* (San Francisco: Harper & Row, Publishers, 1987) pp. 1–25.

ous" oneness of souls or spirits, no matter how much it is committed to the desirability of marital permanency.[2]

Perhaps the most helpful interpretation and reframing of the one-flesh metaphor I have found is in Philip Turner's pamphlet *Divorce: A Christian Perspective*, in which he suggests that becoming one flesh be thought of as forming a particularly close new *society* requiring mutual love and sacrifice, along with the recognition of the continuing particularity of the society's two members. Their beings do not dissolve into one-fleshness along the lines of a theological horror film created by Steven Spielberg. Like all "societies," this one has both its obligations and its requirements for sustenance. When those obligations or requirements cannot be met, the society—like any society—breaks down and dies. In fact, it may be necessary formally to disband the society either to protect its innocent members or to preserve the integrity of the original vow to love and care for the "one flesh."[3]

All of that is clearly consistent with the biblical provisions for divorce, particularly to protect the rights and futures of either man or woman, as the case may be. What strikes me as even more significant is that the "society" image recognizes the flawedness and incompleteness of fallible human beings. We are blessed with the capacity to attempt great things on this earth, and marriage must surely rank as one of them. But we are also reminded, day in and day out, that not all our strivings work. One of the really staggering and hurtful misconceptions about divorce is the assumption we commonly and unknowingly make that somehow *this* striving and venture, unlike any other in the human circus, is denied room for failure and held instead to a counsel of perfection that, in the eyes of many, reaches ontological proportions! If "one flesh" is

[2] Luck, p. 25.

[3] Philip Turner, *Divorce: A Christian Perspective* (Cincinnati: Forward Movement Publications, 1983) pp. 11–13.

taken to mean that, then it has lost its life and joy and become a quasi-religious straitjacket. One may choose to believe that way, but I believe it is important that we recognize there is little biblical warrant for it.

This is also the place to enter a demurrer to the commonly used biblical image of marriage as a "covenant" either between the two partners or between them and God, on the analogy of the covenant found in the Bible between God and God's people. To be sure, the word has an ordinary English meaning something like "contract," though perhaps with a bit more flair, and it is also found in the language of many a marriage ceremony. In connection with the "one flesh" image, the marriage "covenant" is often given the connotation of something sacred and unbreakable, a cut or two above an "agreement," "relationship," or "contract." By calling a marriage a "covenant" we imply a sort of binding mutuality that seems to say that breaking up (or "sundering," in the biblical phrase) such an arrangement has far more cosmic consequences than, for instance, setting aside a contract.

Undeniably the rich texture of the word "covenant" carries a lot of appeal at wedding time, expressing even in its secular use something of the depth of commitment and earnestness of expectation with which (we hope) a marriage will begin. All to the good. The problem, however, is that the *biblical* idea of covenant is much more restricted and specific than our popular use. In the Bible the covenant is a relationship established solely by God with God's people. It is not initiated by those people. They may be faithful or unfaithful *in* the covenant relationship, but they do not have the power to create it. Again and again in the biblical narratives God renews, reinstates, restores, and reestablishes the covenant even though the people have fallen short, wandered after other gods, violated their Lord's expectations, and so on. In short, "covenant" in the

Bible is in no sense a mutual coming together *agreeing* to a relationship. To the contrary, it is God choosing people and asking them to respond. Covenant involves two parties—God and humankind—but it is not *mutual.*

You can begin to see, then, why no matter how wonderful the image may be on other grounds, in terms of what the Bible means, comparing a marital relationship to that of God's covenant just will not work. Marriage is two-sided, and if those two sides can no longer work together, it is over. God's covenant in the Bible is entirely God's work, not a human enterprise. Nothing we do can either affect or abrogate that work. It is another world from that of marriage and divorce. There are marvelous ways of expressing the deep feelings and possibilities of marriage; "covenant," unfortunately, on biblical and theological grounds, is not one of them.

The part that Jesus added to the Genesis image, "What God has joined together let no one put asunder," poses a slightly different question that we will take up again in the next section: "Does Jesus here mean to prohibit divorce?" William Luck notes that Jesus does not here use the familiar and common term for divorce, but chooses another that *never* in the New Testament is used to mean "divorce."[4] The translation "sunder" or "separate" is accurate. The point is that while Jesus is saying that separating this "one flesh" *should* not happen, there is nothing in either the law or metaphysics that says it *cannot.*

---

[4] Luck, pp. 137–38. Luck's argument is fairly ingenious on linguistic grounds, but a reader should realize that he is going against the grain of most biblical scholarship in trying to hear Jesus stop short of an outright prohibition of divorce. He acknowledges that by choosing the word translated "sunder" Jesus calls divorce "immoral," but not "illegal," in order to keep from running afoul of the Pharisees, who would have pounced on the latter as a distortion of Jewish law.

DIVORCE-MADE ADULTERY (MATTHEW 5:31–32, 19:3–10; MARK 10:2–12; LUKE 16:18)

I have to admit that approaching this section of these two chapters has caused me not only more anxious soul-searching but also more scratchy-eyed poring over technical biblical scholarship than any other. The net result is surprisingly simple and straightforward (considering the amount of writing on the subject!): contrary to the Old Testament view, the New Testament is plainly opposed to divorce, period. Particularly for Christian believers, the words of Jesus that head up this section seem to offer not only little comfort but a large dose of condemnation. Jesus is saying, with little ambiguity, that a man who divorces his wife makes her an adulteress and a man who marries a divorced woman commits adultery himself. There is just no way to hear that but as a strong prohibition against divorce. What do we do with that?

I propose we do three things, *because the undeniable surface clarity of the New Testament view still leaves the modern divorcing person with the responsibility and need for deciding how he or she will interpret, construe, feel about, and act on what is said there.* In other words, the story is not over yet. I want to talk about (1) what Jesus actually says, (2) about the meaning of what he says in the original context in which people would have heard and understood it, and (3) about at least one position modern hearers can legitimately take when thinking about the spiritual dimension of their own divorce experience in light of "what the Bible says"—*and does not say.*

THE WORDS OF JESUS

The first thing we have to do is come to some conclusion about what Jesus (and New Testament writers, especially the apostle Paul) *actually say* about divorce, and even a cursory reading of the relevant New Testament texts shows that that is not such an easy task. Though I am not going to pull you through a lot of highly technical textual scholarship, if you are seriously concerned about the New Testament view, there *are* two details that have to be addressed. The first is that the basic single saying of Jesus on the subject of divorce, which occurs in the gospels of Matthew, Mark, and Luke, is found in two forms, and they both cannot be "original." In one form Jesus takes a very hard line: "Everyone who divorces his wife and marries another woman commits adultery, and whoever marries a divorced woman commits adultery, and whoever divorces her husband and marries another man commits adultery." That version appears in Luke 16 and Mark 10. In the version of the same speech that occurs in Matthew 5 and 19, however, a phrase has been added that biblical scholars refer to as "the exception clause." Here Jesus says, "Everyone who divorces his wife *except for immorality* makes her commit adultery, and whoever marries a divorced woman commits adultery." Now the question is, "Do we have any way of telling whether the 'exception clause' is original with Jesus or something the author of the gospel added on?" While a certain number of divorcing people may be rooting for the exception clause ("looking for loopholes," as W. C. Fields is supposed to have retorted when caught reading the Bible!), the weight of biblical scholarship unfortunately goes the other direction: the original "hard" saying of Jesus contains no exception and therefore is even harder than Matthew makes it.

Why this discrepancy should be present in the first place is probably explained by considering the second technical detail. Unfortunately, in some English translations of the Bible that exception clause has been translated "except for *adultery*," leading people naturally to believe that if a wife is adulterous, then Jesus permits divorce. There is a specific Greek term for "adultery," however, which is known and used elsewhere by the author of Matthew; if that author had meant "adultery" here, he would surely have used the correct term. The term that appears here has a recognizable English descendant: it is *porneia*, from the Greek word for prostitution, from which eventually comes our word "pornography," and the best translation of the Greek in context is simply "sexual immorality."

What on earth, then, does "immorality" refer to as Matthew portrays Jesus using it, and why does it get inserted in this gospel? Perhaps the most accurate statement of scholarly consensus on the subject was given to me in conversation by a New Testament scholar colleague of mine, who said, "Who the hell knows?!" Beyond that, though, probably included in the meaning of the term *porneia* is a wide range of pagan sexual practices, *including some that were legal in terms of secular law but forbidden by Jewish religious code.* That difference in legal systems—civil and religious—creates a potentially problematic situation for people who, for instance, were legally married in the eyes of civil law but through conversion entered the domain of a religious law that said their marriage was "immoral." Here, then, a Gentile convert to Christianity (such as would be found, most likely, in the church for which the Gospel of Matthew was originally written) might find him- or herself in a serious conflict if he or she had previously entered into a marriage that was legal by civil standards (for instance, marriage to someone somehow related to you) *but forbidden by Jewish law* (which, keep in mind, still governed most of the lives of the earliest Christian converts). The only way for them to obey Jewish law would be to divorce, *but now along comes Jesus saying that divorce is not permitted!* The "exception clause" is the *church's* solution to the problem. One New Testament scholar has summed the situation up succinctly:

> This Catch-22 leaves such Gentiles in Matthew's church in the awkward position of having to disobey either the LAW by remaining in [forbidden] marriages . . . or Jesus' authority by getting divorced. The pressure of this necessity forges the exceptive clause. Matthew's church remembers Jesus' divorce saying (or reframes it) to retain the essence of the saying but accommodate it to the church's needs. The exceptive clause both keeps Jesus from abrogating Torah (he does not absolutely forbid divorce [which Jewish law permits]) but, as with the other antitheses of the Sermon on the Mount ["You have heard it said . . . but I say unto you"], intensifies and radicalizes Torah and allows Gentiles to obey Jesus.[5]

The same analysis, by the way, accounts for the limited acceptance of divorce on grounds of "immorality" in Paul's letter to the Corinthians (I Cor. 7).

All that has been a mouthful, but I believe it was necessary in order to determine the clearest possible statement of what, with some liberties, might be called "The New Testament position on divorce." If a divorcing person hopes for "permission" or "approval" for divorce *per se* in the New Testament, he or she simply will not find it *in what is actually said.*

THE ORIGINAL SETTING

The second thing we need to do, however, is take very seriously the context in which the words of Jesus (or Paul)

---

[5] Elizabeth Johnson, Ph.D., Assistant Professor of New Testament, New Brunswick Theological Seminary, New Brunswick, N.J., in personal correspondence.

would have been heard, and here two matters of enormous significance for our understanding arise. One is the sad but undisputed fact that in the Jewish culture to which Jesus spoke the rights of women were nearly nil. Women were regarded basically as a form of property, and a woman without a husband found herself in an untenable, maybe even unsurvivable, situation.[6] Jewish law, on either its then strict or more liberal reading, nevertheless permitted men to divorce their wives with ease. Consistent throughout the teaching of Jesus and his followers is his radical concern for people who are "marginal," who have neither right nor regard in a society that cruelly excluded them: the poor, sinners, the diseased, the outcast, *and women*. Scholars agree that his teaching on divorce, even more than being a commentary on marriage, is a radical and even revolutionary statement of the rights of women: they cannot be cast off by their husbands like a garden tool that no longer works.

Notwithstanding the ongoing need for concern about women's rights and roles in society today, things now stand very differently, both legally and religiously. The "hardness" of the New Testament view of divorce has to be heard today in a very different context, and its force as an influence in our own thinking and acting will naturally be correspondingly different.

The second aspect of the New Testament context is probably even more important for our understanding of what it says about divorce. Unfortunately, this is an element that, while well-known to biblical scholars and a part of their everyday working assumption, is often unknown or misunderstood by lay people. There are lots of regrettable gaps of knowledge between the scholarly and the popular worlds, but this one is particularly destructive

---

[6] A good scholarly summary of much of this material is to be found in Wolfgang Schrage, *The Ethics of the New Testament* (tr. David E. Green) (Philadelphia: Fortress Press, 1988) pp. 91 ff.

for divorcing people seeking guidance about the spiritual dimensions of their situation. Jesus and the early church confidently believed that the "end of the age" was at hand, and that the world, as then known, would vanish in the coming of the Kingdom of God. To put it technically, they lived and thought in terms of an "apocalyptic world view," arranging their lives, values, and practices according to the expectation that God would soon appear to conduct the last judgment and inaugurate the new age of the Kingdom.

Given that apocalyptic assumption, it was incumbent on believers to prepare themselves for the coming of the Kingdom and to be as pure and blameless as possible when the day arrived. A true believer would have held him- or herself to the special standards of ritual purity required of priests and holy warriors, *which not only did not permit divorce but were equally skittish about marriage itself and any form of sexual activity.* Certain ascetic communities in the New Testament world—the Essenes at Qumran, for instance—had made this ritual preparedness a dominant lifestyle and religious demand. There is ample evidence that Jesus himself exhorts his hearers to more stringent and restrictive living than even the sternest Jewish law required because he, too, spoke from the perspective of an apocalyptic world view that saw the end as near.

That is why the New Testament displays its traditionally "un-Jewish" skepticism not only about divorce but also about marriage and sexuality of any kind: the believer must be prepared and pure for the coming end, a matter of being "fit for the Kingdom" in Jesus' words. The Christian was not permitted to divorce not so much because it was against the law of God (which in the traditional Jewish understanding it clearly was *not*) but because of the special requirements for the coming Kingdom. That, in other words, is the source and rationale for the otherwise clear position the New Testament takes.

What force that position has for a person today depends correspondingly on how fully they share the same apocalyptic world view. Much of the later development of the still early church, even within the later writings of the New Testament, had to do with coming to terms, both theologically and experientially, with the soon undeniable "delay" of the expected Kingdom, and ultimately with coming to new and revised understandings of what, in actual fact, that whole idea meant and what it would be like.

It is also important to keep in mind that although the New Testament writers represent Jesus as forbidding divorce, the church itself, as it came to terms with its misunderstanding of the imminence of the coming Kingdom, accepted it from the very earliest period. Matthew's "exception clause," as well as Paul's provision for divorce from unbelievers in I Corinthians 7, are examples within the New Testament itself. In point of fact, *every* culture and religion has made *some* provision for the dissolution of unsatisfactory marriages.

AN HONEST UNDERSTANDING FOR TODAY

After all the technical biblical scholarship is done (and it has been considerable, I assure you), we can now come to the third and final part of this section, the question of what positions a modern divorcing person can legitimately take on the question of the New Testament view of divorce. My aim here is not so much to sell you on a particular position, as to help us gain some clarity not only about the complexity of the subject but also about what informed and well-meaning people can legitimately adopt as a posture about their own divorce experience *should they choose to look at it taking Jesus' words as normative.*

Perhaps it is obvious by now that I myself am by no

means of the "literalist" disposition when it comes to biblical interpretation. But more than that, it is important to recognize that people under stress *tend to become literal* about lots of things—whether it is the meaning of authoritative writings (the Bible or your favorite cookbook) or "signs in the stars." (I recall with a mixture of embarrassment and humor a time years ago when I was making a long, fatiguing drive under icy winter weather conditions and had to stop at a motel because the roads were so slick. In my relief and exhaustion, and with a little playfulness, I grabbed the ever present Gideon Bible and let it fall open to a scripture at random, which happened to be from one of the Psalms, "Trust in the Lord and thou shalt not *slide*"! Some tiny, literalist part of me at that moment swallowed it hook, line, and sinker!) I have listened to divorcing people who were not otherwise anywhere close to a literalist or fundamentalist position on the Bible agonize about the *precise* words of scripture as they might apply to their situations. The problem here is not really literalism, however, so much as what we would do better to call *atomism*— taking isolated bits of scripture out of their contexts and their relation to the biblical *ideas and meanings* that the writers are trying to express. I believe it is important for us to tell divorcing people that they do not *have* to do that about divorce any more than they would have to about any of the other bits of scripture that, taken as "atoms," become absurd—women keeping silent in church, for instance, or people plucking their eyes out when they see something nasty.

The position I come to therefore is that if one of the strong ideas of the New Testament is its apocalyptic belief in the perfecting of creation at the end of the age, an even stronger one is that creation *prior* to that is imperfect, "sinful," and in need of restoration by a loving and forgiving God. No, neither Jesus nor the earliest church *wanted* marriages to end in divorce, any more than anyone today wants that agony, no matter how much of a relief it may eventually turn out to be. But I also know that the final word of scripture is not about broken covenants but renewed ones, not about judgment but about mercy, not about falling away from a wrathful God but being gathered up in the arms of a loving one.

So far as the "hard saying" itself that kicked off this discussion is concerned, I do not believe I have any really honest choice but to take a "guilty as charged" position, but not to feel either condemned or overwhelmed by it. Such a view says, in essence, "Though there may be some confusion about the actual meaning and current application of Jesus' term 'sexual immorality,' the plain fact is that I have failed in what was my intention for marriage, and in, as best I can understand it, what was God's. I rely now on the rest of what Jesus said and offered about forgiveness and new beginnings, without trying to reduce the seriousness and hurtfulness of my divorce, both for me and my ex-spouse. What the New Testament says about divorce is both time-bound and locked in a world view few today share; it is in no sense a binding moral judgment for today's context. The main message of Jesus is elsewhere, and that is my primary source of guidance and self-understanding." One might also add that, considering the current rate of extramarital sexual involvement in at least American society—well over 50 percent for men and nearly that for women—"adultery" as a label is not exactly at the top of the extraordinary or life-threatening list. If, in other words, divorcing even without any hint of infidelity in the marriage itself makes me a species of "adulterer," then I join the already rather large ranks of those who need redemption.

Though I believe the "guilty as charged" position to be the most honest one, both biblically and psychologically, there are several others one might take, each of which has at least something worth knowing and considering. Let me describe them briefly:

First, there is the "straight talk" understanding, meaning that we take Jesus' words at their actual face value, leaving aside such nuances as cultural or terminological differences. That means, to put the matter bluntly, that the following situations are "covered" by one (though not all) of these four texts: (1) if you are a man and divorce your wife for any reason except her sexual immorality (for which divorce is permitted without consequence), then that makes her an adulteress if and when she remarries; (2) if you are a man and divorce your wife for any reason whatever, then that makes her an adulteress (a tension between what Jesus says in Luke and Matthew compared to Mark); (3) if you are a man, divorce your wife either for any reason (Luke and Mark) or for infidelity (Matthew) and then remarry, you commit adultery yourself; (4) if you are a woman and divorce your husband for any allowable reason and remarry, you commit adultery; and (5) if you are a man and marry a divorced woman, you commit adultery.

There are two obvious problems with the "straight talk" understanding. One is that the New Testament writers have Jesus saying things that contradict Jewish law, so that which of the sayings he in fact meant—the limited or unlimited categories, one might say—makes a great deal of difference. The second difficulty is that, again depending on which verse you read, not all current divorcing situations are addressed, leaving some of us up in the air. You may, of course, opt to dissolve these differences and simply say that people who are divorced commit adultery when they remarry, and cause their ex-spouses to do the same, period.

Second, there is the "consider the source" understanding, which notices that Jesus' sayings are in two places placed in the context of an argument with Pharisees over a rather technical point of Jewish divorce law, but are not necessarily intended to be normative "teachings" about the practice of faithful followers. More to the point, the primary concern is over Jesus' authority. Scholars note, for instance, that the full force of what Jesus says is to undergird the mostly neglected rights of women, who according to one school of rabbinical thought at the time could be divorced for any displeasure whatever they caused their husbands. On this view, the weight of Jesus' remarks is essentially to say, "But if you do that, consider the consequences for her well-being and standing in the community." Perhaps even more important in this understanding is the belief that no isolated saying of Jesus (or any other biblical text, for that matter) can be fully understood or applied without taking the whole belief structure of which it is a part into account. For Christians, that would mean saying that the Gospel is not a series of sayings or rules but rather a total cosmic event in which the God of the universe became incarnate in the man Jesus, and that both our and the biblical writers' understandings and perceptions of that event are inescapably flawed and limited. In any case, it is the total significance of the Gospel that impacts my life, gives it direction, and provides the moral framework within which I take responsibility for my decisions and actions.

Third, there is the "culture shock" understanding, which says, in effect, that both marital standards and the meaning and significance of "adultery" in biblical times were so different from ours that no direct application of the text is possible. For instance, Jesus limits his appellation of "adultery" to a *remarriage* situation, not to sexual relationship outside of marriage. Further, this position would note the disciples' apparently horrified reaction to what Jesus says —"Who then wants to take a chance on marriage?"—and his almost acid comeback in Matthew and Mark to the effect that if the risk is too great you can always become a self-made eunuch and avoid marriage altogether! This understanding would say that no matter how faithfully we exercise our Christian faith and belief in Jesus in other areas, these sayings are made irrelevant by both inaccuracy in transmission ("What did the man actually say anyway, since we have some irreconcilable choices before us?") and cultural difference ("Sleeping with another woman is not adulterous, only marrying her"). Perhaps an even more important consideration has to do with the role of marriage in society in biblical times as compared to now. In those days survival in society as a single adult person was far less possible than today (unless you were very wealthy); the importance of being part of somebody's "household" (for economic and other reasons) was vastly greater then than now. The stringency of marital law at that time, both religious and secular, has to do then with the greater dependence of the social order on both the durability and universality of marriage as an institution.

A fourth possible position could be called the "what's in a name?" understanding, raising serious questions about the meaning of the term "adultery," both as it is translated from the Greek and as it was utilized in the culture. A strong case can be made, for instance, that Jesus meant nonsexual adultery, intending to point to the gravity of the divorcing situation but not to the more tightly defined legal category of marital infidelity.[7] "Adultery" in that sense is still not a good thing, mind you, but the word may be used analogously to the way we use the word "steal" when actual, illegal theft is not the meaning—as when we say that someone "absolutely stole" something. Here, too, one would wonder what weight and significance "adultery" even of a sexual type had in the culture of its day. Was it more or less damning than it is today, for instance? What about the cultural difference that allowed Israel to keep on its books the death penalty for women adulterers, but let men go scot-free and, for the most part, not even

[7] Luck, p. 61.

call their extramarital liaisons "adultery" (not to mention the polygamy that was entirely legal through much of the Old Testament period)? People taking this position would accept responsibility for the gravity of their divorcing situation, but would not feel themselves "charged" with a crime in any precise moral or legal sense.

THE CLEAR WORD OF RESTORATION

I have taken into account several different ways of reading the Bible in these pages, while at the same time saying candidly that *how* one reads it (one's hermeneutical approach) has a great deal to do with *what* one will hear it actually saying. I also have to say, however, that I believe anyone who enters the Bible's pages hunting primarily for literal rules for living and decision-making, or for God's direct commentary about individual life situations such as divorce, will emerge disappointed, frustrated, and confused. The "truth" of the Bible is seldom, if ever, to be found in any one passage, episode, or least of all saying. We may say, on scholarly grounds, that it is *true* that, as best we can tell, Jesus said what he did about divorce to the Pharisees and to his disciples. If we stopped there, however, or took that to be the whole truth of either the Bible's or Jesus' own message, we would have not only a bleak but also a distorted picture. It is only by looking at the much wider view that the truth emerges, and if I can risk summing it up in a single thought it would be this: the Bible presents the belief of religious people over a span of thousands of years that the transcendent God seeks broken and wandering human beings to restore them to wholeness and the depth of membership in creation for which we reserve the special word "communion" —with each other, with themselves, and with that same God. That basic message is refined in different religious cultures, Jewish or Christian, for instance, but essentially it is the same. Here is the consistently clear word about divorce to be found in scripture: we who have experienced the brokenness of divorce are sought by a God who is bent on restoring us, not condemning us or putting us through a moral CAT scan. If, in the Bible's terms, there are aspects of our divorcing situation that call for repentance, then we are clearly summoned to that—but only for the purpose of restoration. If we believe ourselves victims in the divorcing process, we are called away from either blame or self-pity into restoration.

When I work with Christian divorcing people who are worried about what Jesus either says or seems to say about divorce, I often say that the most important New Testament passages to look at "on the subject" are such episodes as his encounter with the Samaritan woman (John 4:7–26) or with the men about to stone a woman caught in adultery (John 8:3–11) or with the tax collector Zacchaeus (Luke 19:1–10). "But they're not about *divorce*" people say. "Not true," I reply, "they are about the only thing that really matters in coming to terms with your divorce, and that is confronting a failure and a sense of loss, and maybe even a great wrongdoing, and being offered a new future. They are about how both God's will and human brokenness meet in the miracle of restoration, and *that* is the Bible's clear word about divorce."

EIGHT

Forgiveness Has Its Limits

SHE WAS GONE AGAIN. He had noticed a few more of the warning signs this time—the edginess, the tone of voice, the canceled evening out—but not enough completely to deflect the now familiar sharp blow to the chest that her sudden, angry departures always caused. He was a fool and knew it, for all the good it did. A year before their marriage he had fallen in love with her, a beautiful, fey woman whose inner torments only made her more attractive to him. The shape of the roller coaster they rode was now starkly familiar on his emotional horizon. First would come a blissful time of shared passion and inner closeness the likes of which he had rarely experienced before. They would make plans, and playfully but carefully handle the artifacts of their earlier courtship: the special place, the private code, the silly gift, the public dare of being a couple. Their hours together would be punctuated by those earnest discussions and revelations of the heart that always seemed unparalleled to them, no matter how often repeated. They would savor the unfolding of their relationship, unique to them in all the universe, from the "what-ifs" to the "won't-it-be-wonderfuls."

Then the fear would begin to creep in and she would be "too busy," "need some space," "talk to you later," a litany of withdrawal, ending, most often, with an angry, "I can't do this anymore," and if not outright departure, at best silence. That was the worst of it: the silence that always left him wondering what *he* had done (little, if anything, he could ever discover) and where she had *gone* (even in the times when she physically stayed and he saw her every day). In time, he had learned, the silence would be broken and she would acknowledge him again, return as wife and lover, abundantly sorry for the pain she had inflicted, incredulously grateful for his patience in waiting for her, committed anew to making it work this time. And so it would begin again, a little better than the time before, just enough to let him believe they would make it now, his anger and hurt dissolving in a new wave of love and forgiveness and, yes, hope. But soon, much too soon . . .

Some variation of that story plays through many a divorce. It is a story about one of the most deeply held values in human relationships, whether on religious or purely secular terms: the need for and the virtue of *forgiveness.* When we are taught from an early age to forgive even our enemies, it is a moral certainty that forgiveness will be high on the list of things we should aim for with our spouses and lovers. Sometimes we mean the word in a strict moral sense, as in forgiving someone a wrong done to us. Often, too, however, we broaden it out a bit to include those times when there is not a question of moral wrongdoing but rather one of sticking with someone through shortcomings, failures, or painful behavior that affects us. I am using the term to cover both kinds of meaning; the personal dynamics are much the same even when the exact situations are not.

Without forgiveness the world would clearly be a sorry place and human relationships would be in a shambles most of the time. The alternatives to forgiveness in relationships are not at all promising: either life becomes a moral point system, where you may be allowed a certain number of failings but when you reach your limit the jig is up, like losing your driver's license or having a radiation detection badge turn whatever color it does just before you go up in smoke; or, on the other hand, life may become a complicated minuet of denial in which negativity and wrongdoing must be pretended (or rationalized) out of existence because we have no way of compensating for them. Forgiveness means we do not have either to keep score or to whistle in the dark. Forgiveness allows relationships to endure and even grow from the failings and weaknesses of their partners. Openly acknowledging the pain one has suffered or caused and forgiving or being forgiven its consequences can be one of the most deeply feeling and nourishing times in any relationship. Popularity aside, Erich Segal is surely wrong in *Love Story* that love means never having to say I'm sorry.[1] It is in the "I'm sorry"/"you're forgiven" times that people come together at new levels of understanding, commitment to each other, and personal responsibility for what they mean and do together. (I am convinced, for instance, that one reason

[1] Erich Segal, *Love Story* (New York: Harper & Row, Publishers, 1970).

adolescent love is so important is that it can teach young people something that otherwise seems strikingly absent from the teenage repertoire, at least as I experience it daily: the ability to say—and mean—"I'm sorry, please forgive me.")

People in divorce, however, often have a more painfully self-conscious and troubled experience with forgiveness, to the point that sooner or later a question we usually try to push away elbows its way into the picture: *How much forgiveness is enough anyway?* It is not a very pleasant question, but I hear divorcing people agonizing a lot about it, and not getting much help in the process of trying to answer. That is the aim of this chapter. The woman whose husband has once again left behind telltale evidence of infidelity asks it; the man who carries his wife to bed again after another bout with the gin bottle asks it; the earnest lover whose spouse has pulled away yet again asks it. In fact, I think we all ask it: does forgiveness have its limits? Is there a point at which on spiritual and moral grounds the permitted, *even best*, choice is to draw the line and *stop* forgiving? And even though it goes down hard with many of us nurtured on the absolute, even divine, goodness of forgiveness, the answer, which I want to make no bones about, is *yes*.

The question, of course, is how does one know when enough is enough, when to invoke the famous dictum attributed to W. C. Fields, "If at first you don't succeed, try, try again. If you still don't succeed, forget it—there's no point making a damn fool of yourself." But there is more: even if we can somehow find a legitimate way to shake off the perfectionistic ethic of *always* forgiving turning the other cheek, going the second mile, and more, there remains the question of how do I *know* when the cutoff point is reached and the time has come to decide—to end a marriage or relationship, to change my pattern of interaction with a former spouse, to do anything differently from "taking it" and hoping, hoping, hoping that things will change. That is the twofold agenda of this chapter: learning to acknowledge that forgiveness has its limits and learning to know when enough is enough.

It has taken me a long time to admit that this side of heaven what we usually think of as "forgiveness" is not absolute—neither always possible nor always healthy— and still longer to reconcile it with the spiritual value system I was raised with and hold deeply as my own. The struggle continues, and in a paradoxical way I have come to be thankful for it because that is what makes divorcing a journey rather than a disaster. In this subject, as in many that divorcing people live with, the difference is between finding *an answer* and learning to live with an ongoing, back-and-forth *process*. I suspect many, if not most of us, start out searching for the former, and gradually discover that what we get—ultimately to our betterment—is the latter.

Let me illustrate the difference with something of an aside before going on with the question of forgiveness itself. There are two kinds of "questions" in the world, logically speaking, and correspondingly two kinds of "answers." One kind of question is the one for which you can (at least theoretically) get a clear chunk of resolution that ends the matter. How far away is the sun? Ninety-three million miles. Is it wrong to murder somebody? Yes. Can I have the car tomorrow night, Dad? No. The other kind of question, though, does not get clear-cut factual responses so much as *directions to a way of living*. These are the questions to which the only appropriate answer is "yes and no," which means that to live with the question I am going to have to learn to live with some degree of uncertainty, of switching back and forth between one pole and its opposite, of what in philosophical terms we would call "dialectic." What is important is being sure that the right kind of response gets hooked up to the matching kind of question, that when you are holding on to tab A you hunt for slot A, not slot B. The sun is an answerable distance away, but is the sun friend or foe of human beings? Ah, the only answer here has to be "it depends." With too little I do not have enough vitamin D to survive, but with too much I can get bad sunburn or skin cancer. The answer is a direction to a way of living—with the sun.

Many of the questions that arise in human relationships, including divorce, may appear at first to be of the first type but are really of the second, and a lot of confusion about relationships comes from mixing them up and trying to stuff tab A into slot B. When people ask, for instance, "Is divorce wrong?" or "Does divorce hurt children?" expecting to get an answer of the first sort, they are setting themselves up for terminal confusion and frustration, because down deep those are the *other* kind of question. You will not realistically find "an answer" for them (though some religious or ethical systems try), but you can discover something about living in a process with them. When I think about some aspects of the family life my children will never have because their parents are divorced, I may feel, "It's wrong; they're hurt." But if I think about how much of my parental energy was tapped off in marital disharmony and denied them before, things look very different. The trick is that I have to be able to think both ways, take ownership of both feelings, and acknowledge that my experience is a mixture of gains and losses. What I get as an "answer" then is some direction for living with that back-and-forth dialectical process in a way that moves me forward on life's journey toward love and responsibility.

Or take, for example, the matters of control and dependence in relationships. We sometimes say of people that they are "very controlling" or "very dependent," as though the idea were that one should stop being one or the other. In point of fact, however, I am a mixture of both.

Sometimes I want (and need) to take control and other times I want (and need) to depend on someone else. The trick is learning *how* to be both things (which human beings undeniably are) so that one side or the other appears at the right time and under the right circumstances, in a healthy interaction with my "other's" parallel experience and nature. If we are both on the controlling side or both in a dependency mode at the same time, we have got trouble; or if one of us is so dominantly one or the other and vice versa that we cannot exchange roles when appropriate, then the relationship may be fatally skewed.

All of this has been intended to get us to the right angle for getting some purchase on the "question" of forgiveness. It is an issue of the second type, not the first, and that makes all the difference. Does forgiveness have its limits? How much forgiveness is enough? The answer I thought was being taught me by both the spiritual and the cultural values with which I was raised was wrong because it mistook the type of question it was. It said, in essence, that there should be no limit to forgiveness, that because God never stops forgiving we should not either, and that if I found myself unable to forgive in a given instance I had no choice but to mark it up as a moral failing on my part. About relationships in particular it sometimes pointed to the Old Testament prophet Hosea, whose life story was held up as a picture of how God operates and a model of what we should strive for. In the story Hosea keeps forgiving his wandering, prostitute wife Gomer, taking her back and loving her when both the law and the culture's expectation clearly told him to throw in the towel and divorce her. That is the way God treats Israel, the book says, and its readers over the centuries have echoed that that is how we should aim to treat each other, too. In general that position pointed to Jesus' response in the New Testament (Mt. 18:22 and Lk. 17:4) when he was asked how often we should forgive and gave the cryptic reply "seventy times seven," which in the symbolic idiom of the ancient Near East would not have meant 490 times, but essentially limitless numbers.

The real answer is different, however, and neither nearly so easy nor so guilt-producing. Hosea was talking about the infinite love of God, and Jesus was talking about the Kingdom of Heaven. I hope to enjoy the former and enter the latter, but regrettably my love is not transcendent and the Kingdom is not real estate I own. The far better answer is an invitation to and a direction for a process of thinking about and living with your situation. The answer will take you on a journey of thought and spirit, of reflection and feeling, which is what I am trying to say divorce *can* be if we let it.

Before we get more specific about what limiting forgiveness means, however, we do have to be clear about what is involved in "forgiving" to begin with, because the very language of forgiveness can get slippery. In both common and theological usage "forgiveness" means either or both of two things. First, forgiveness can be an internal attitude or feeling that in some rather mysterious way turns loose of the sense of having been wronged or indebted. When I forgive someone for something in this internal way, the sense of being "owed," so to speak, changes, and the feelings of hurt and anger that typically accompanied whatever happened shift, even if they do not vanish altogether ("forgiving" is most assuredly *not* the same as "forgetting," nor should it produce any such amnesia, lest people fail to learn from their mistakes). Second, however, forgiveness can also be an external act of setting aside certain of the otherwise likely or appropriate consequences of someone's behavior. In this mode I may decide not to do something about the offending behavior that I otherwise would have done and that it would have been appropriate to have done. Here is the sense, for instance, in which we speak of a financial debt being "forgiven," meaning that the person who owes the money no longer has to pay it back. Relationally speaking, I may decide to resume activity with someone instead of cutting it off. I have scratched my head quite a lot about the question of whether genuine forgiveness can take *either but not both* of those forms, and finally decided it probably cannot: there must be both an internal reorientation of feeling and *some* external acting out of that new perspective. That is the same one-two operation on the part of the forgiver that we require (on theological grounds, for instance) of the offender: both an internal change ("confession" or being sorry) and an external demonstration ("repentance" or making reparations).

Notice, though, something very tricky about the whole business: if you examine your own experience of forgiving, you will quickly see that forgiveness in the internal sense does not mean there are *no* outward consequences, and forgiveness in the external sense does not mean there are no remaining feelings, though both consequences and feelings may be different from what they would have been had forgiveness not taken place. What essentially happens in forgiveness is that a personal connectedness that had been threatened is now restored, and the "flow" of the interaction or relationship resumes. *When we choose not to forgive, the most important thing we are doing is declining that reconnection and re-flow.* When I speak of the limits of forgiveness, I am certainly not talking about holding a grudge or waging a vendetta or, still worse, righteously stroking one's grievance in self-pity. It is more like achieving an emotional neutrality inwardly and a relational disengagement outwardly. The point of the decision to limit forgiveness is to bring an end to what we do that, in effect, permits and perpetuates negative behavior in, from, and for the other person.

Having said all that, I would now like to suggest five guidelines or ways of thinking about the forgiveness issue.

Going through divorce may bring them to the surface after long submersion. They are about (1) boundaries, about (2) recognizing limitations in relationships, about (3) what tolerance means—and does not mean, about (4) the question of incompatibility in a relationship, and about (5) the utterly nonromantic destructiveness of a lost cause.

FORGIVENESS ON THE BOUNDARIES

I speak often in these pages about the vital importance of establishing and cultivating appropriate personal boundaries. With the subject of forgiveness, the idea of boundaries once again can give us an operating principle and a perspective from which to look at ourselves that is psychologically honest but also spiritually sensitive. Return for a minute to the man with whom this chapter opened—an actual case I worked closely with over a long period of time. Looked at from one angle, his faithful waiting for his wife's return was a shining example of forgiveness—the "Gomer Syndrome," we could say. How many times should he let himself get pushed around like that? Not an easy thing to say, especially when he was deeply in love with the woman, and also when each time she would cycle back through his life he could see *some* improvement in things—in her own emotional condition, in their interaction, even in the ways they would talk about and work through their previous painful experience. She would be repentant, genuinely sorry about what she had done. What more could one ask?

Well, quite a lot, when you come right down to it. From another angle, you see, that of boundaries, things did not look nearly so good. Her own personal boundaries were in a state of siege much of the time (which is why she got so frightened and kept running away), and his boundaries, though far stronger in a psychic sense, were nevertheless constantly being pummeled and compromised as he waited through her emotional betrayals time and again. The operating question I want us to learn to ask about a given instance of forgiveness is *whether it contributes to the strengthening of personal boundaries both within and between members of a couple.* In the case at hand it simply did not. The man was doing far too much of the "work" of the relationship, leaving his partner free to take flight when the going got rough, without much sense of either the consequences or her personal responsibility. His forgiveness was, in effect, contributing to the erosion of her personal boundaries, to say nothing of his own and of the boundaries of the relationship itself.

Here I suggest that we adopt much the same principle we use in working with friends and families of alcoholics or other substance abusers, trying to teach them that anything they do in the name of love or helpfulness that puts a protective barrier between the alcoholic and the realistic consequences of his or her drinking is not helpful at all but quite the reverse because it blurs rather than highlights the person's boundaries.

Though she did not use the word "forgiveness," a woman in a physically abusive relationship was caught in much the same trap. Because her spouse beat up on her while he was drunk and remembered little of it after it was over, she felt guilty about leaving him. She was, he said, the best thing that had ever happened to him and he would be lost without her. What she slowly had to realize was that in terms of having functional personal boundaries he was really quite lost *with* her, and her pretending it just was not so was not helping matters at all.

Your situation is probably different from these brief vignettes, but I still believe it is possible to ask as a rule of thumb question whether forgiving a person their behavior is helping strengthen the boundaries of who you, the other, and the two of you together really are. If it is not, then "enough" has been reached. It is time both internally and externally to "disconnect," whether that applies to a particular aspect of someone's behavior, or in the extreme case of divorce to the entire relationship itself.

RECOGNIZING LIMITATIONS IN RELATIONSHIPS

A second rule of thumb for forgiveness has to do with something I daresay hardly any of us either wants to or can do when starting a marriage: sizing up what the potential of the relationship is in terms of what it can and cannot be. Most of us want it to be the ultimate and believe there is no mountain too big to be moved on the way to making it so. (I have yet to see, for instance, a person successfully talked out of getting married by even the closest friends or associates who had plenty of good evidence that going ahead with it would prove a disaster. We just do not think that way. That is one reason why as a minister I do not refuse to perform weddings on grounds that I see the relationship as heading for trouble. That couple is almost surely going to get married by someone, and if I am the person, then maybe I will have a chance to be a pastor to them when—even if I cannot say "if"—the going gets rough.)

As time goes by, however, evidence undeniably begins to accumulate about what the realistic limitations of the relationship are. Probably the easiest illustration of that (though not by any means its most important dimension) is the question of physical appearance. I do not imagine very many newlyweds would say that their bride or groom is unattractive, but a great many have a mental checklist of little repairs and tune-ups they hope will get made before too long. One day the reality may set in that they are not going to happen, and that what you see is pretty much what you get. The weight to be lost or gained, or the fashion sense to be enhanced, or the physical mannerisms that grate, are just there: they constitute a limit on what the relationship is going to be in that department.

Here, for instance, is a woman of considerable talent and professional pride whose husband, while an entirely capable and pleasing person in his own right, simply cannot stand for his wife to accomplish something or be the object of anyone's praise. He refuses to address that problem in either individual or marital therapy, and again and again when his wife does something well he either puts her down or withdraws into his own world. For years she has "forgiven" him and tried to reduce her visibility in things that would threaten him. Again and again she has hoped that by doing so he would be sufficiently reassured to change. Now she has come to see that, given her husband's makeup and his unwillingness to undertake a therapeutic experience that might (or might not) make for substantial change, their relationship has some clear limitations. It is now her choice what she wants to do about them, but I am arguing that she is under no ethical or spiritual obligation to keep "forgiving" her husband by throttling back her own creativity (and, coincidentally, making herself ill in the process with stifled rage and unfulfillment). Or to put it differently, what she must see is that this "forgiving" is not going to change those limitations, and so far as *that* goes, "enough" has been reached. Recognizing the limits of the relationship gives her a tool to use now in assessing the appropriate limits of forgiveness. Let me emphasize that this particular woman, or someone else in a different situation, may appropriately decide that, given the limitations of their relationship, it is right and good to proceed. That is not the point. The point is that forgiveness that blinds us to limitations has no warrant on spiritual grounds.

THE MEANING AND ABUSE OF TOLERANCE

Years ago I remember a seminary professor commenting that the periods in history that were characterized by the greatest religious tolerance were also those of the weakest religious commitment. It was a paradox, sometimes a tragic one historically, that the two seemingly could not occur together. I believe the same thing happens all too often on the personal level, though here I do *not* believe it has to be a paradox we are stuck with. *The rule of thumb I am after is this: when the tolerance that lies behind forgiveness is at the expense of commitment, then the limits of forgiveness have been reached.* I am thinking here fundamentally of the difference between forgiving a spouse's shortcomings or failings because one is committed to the person and the relationship and it is a price willingly (if sometimes dearly) paid, and on the other hand going along with those negatives because in terms of the inner life of the relationship the forgiving person just does not give a damn. In short, what I am arguing is that tolerance does not appropriately mean swallowing all kinds of negative behavior or situations when there is no underlying commitment to back it up and give it meaning and congruence. *Apathetic* tolerance, I would say, is tolerance abused, in the same way that saying "I forgive you" when what the person did made not a dent in my life to begin with is a spiritual deceit.

In a variation on the same theme, it may just be that the *in*tolerance that signals reaching the limits of forgiveness is an expression of very deep commitment of another kind —perhaps to what one believes in as the possibility of a loving relationship for oneself or even for a spouse one can no longer stay with; or perhaps to one's children and the character of their family life. I am thinking here of a woman who fairly early on saw the limitations of her relationship with a husband who in terms of emotional openness, social awareness, and personal maturity was always going to be several leagues behind her. He was, however, sexually faithful, a good provider, and an adequate moral model for their children. She committed herself deeply and completely to being a good mother (her therapist later observed that that included her husband!) and as long as that was working she was a model of toleration, forgiving one after another of her husband's slights, rudenesses, or impetuous outbursts. The day came, however, when her children were raised and she faced at mid-life the growing strength of another commitment altogether: to the possibilities of a fulfilling career for herself, against the wishes of the husband who had never thought of her beyond her cherished mother role, and to life as a single person (though not ruling out the possibility of finding a man she could love and respect and expect the same in return from). Her toleration of her husband waned rapidly and they were divorced. Their friends and family were shocked: how could this woman who had been so patient and forgiving for twenty-five years of marriage suddenly stop being so? Had it all been a sham before, leading to a terminal weariness in well-doing now that the kids were gone? No, not at all. In another case, of course, it *might* have been something like that, but not here. Here a lifetime of commitment and tolerance had gone hand in hand, congruently and on the whole rewardingly. The woman was neither martyr nor self-pitying victim. It was not that her commitment had *changed* so much as that it had been *completed*, now to be replaced by a commitment of a different sort. And that new commitment made her quite *in*tolerant of what she had for good reason put up with before. We might fault that relationship on all kinds of grounds in the best of all worlds, but the point here is that the woman had used the tolerance/commitment rule of thumb effectively and responsibly to assess the limits of her "forgiving" behavior.

Here, by the way, is where the religious and biblical picture of forgiveness can be used again by way of comparison. The ever forgiving behavior of God portrayed in the Bible (with Israel in the covenant and with the church in the life, death, and believed-in resurrection of Jesus Christ) is a tolerance which comes from ultimate, transcendent commitment on God's part. It is, one could say, the paradigm of the partnership between tolerance and commitment, and both Jewish and Christian affirmations are that it costs God dearly and is not something we human beings can successfully imitate, no matter how much we try to let our lives be guided by it. Nowhere in either the Bible or in Christian or Jewish religious tradition are human beings called or expected to match God's faithfulness. We *are* called to respond to it—partly in acknowledging our imperfection and seeking forgiveness or restoration and partly in taking that divine loving-kindness as the compass for our own conduct of living, knowing full well that the iron of our own inadequacies is forever going to pull it at least slightly off course.

THE MYTH AND THE TRUTH OF INCOMPATIBILITY

One of the most oft-heard grounds for marital dissolution is "incompatibility." I fear the term has grown weak and watery with overuse, and what really ought to be a thunderously serious judgment rolls off the tongue after the latest marital spat or midnight uproar over the position of the toilet seat. The rule of thumb I am proposing here is that *genuine* incompatibility signals an appropriate limit for forgiveness, but it first requires that we rescue that word from the inflation it has suffered in common use.

I remember vividly learning a lesson on the subject when I was a teenager, from an adult friend who influenced me greatly in many ways and nursed me through at least one disastrous adolescent love affair. She was describing her own marriage (her second) and at one point said in her inimitably straight-from-the-hip way, "You know this business of couples needing to be compatible is bullshit. Don and I are 'incompatible' in nearly every way I can think of. We don't like the same things, our interests are wildly different, we disagree on nearly every public issue, and if either of us succeeded in raising our kids entirely the way we wanted to, the other would commit murder. Don't let 'em kid you about compatibility, because we are crazy in love and have the strongest marriage I know." Twenty-five years later that is still true, as I know from them firsthand! The point is that *differences do not equate to incompatibility, and compatibility does not consist in spouses making themselves over in the other's image.*

Philip Turner, whose excellent monograph on divorce I cited in the previous chapter, points out that all too often marriages are "fair trade agreements" in which the aim is for each partner to satisfy his or her own needs for fulfillment in what he calls "possessive individualism."[2] On the surface that may *look* like true love and devotion; what is missing down deep, however, is the mutual commitment to creating a new "society" (of two) that is what "one flesh" genuinely means. In the absence of that commitment personal differences easily threaten to derail the project of getting each partner's needs met, and so they turn into what the couple believe are "incompatibilities" or "irreconcilable differences." In fact, however, the culprit in such cases is not difference at all, but rather the

---

[2] Philip Turner, *Divorce: A Christian Perspective* (Cincinnati: Forward Movement Publications) p. 7.

misguided expectations of "possessive individualism." If instead the partners saw their work as contributing perhaps richly different things to the emerging "new society" of their relationship, the compatibility question would look very different.

A corollary point is that "compatibility" that is a sort of turning oneself inside out to match the other's expectations is a sham. Turner writes, for instance:

> If by implication we promise to be compatible with our husband or wife, we by implication also undertake to make ourselves over into the image our spouse may have of us. If this observation is correct then the promises implied by our views of marriage appear similar to the writing of a blank check on another's behalf. To say I will be compatible is to say I will become what you demand. Anyone who makes such a promise or writes such a check stands a good chance of being left with nothing.[3]

We have, then, a common use—misuse, I would say—of the terms "incompatible" and "compatible" that I want to be clear I do *not* mean in this rule of thumb about forgiveness. The presence of even extreme *difference* need not total out to incompatibility, and the attempt to conform to the other's image does not yield compatibility. Having said that, we can get back to what the words should genuinely mean: the occurrence in a relationship of sufficiently pervasive, crucial, and crippling conflictedness to keep the "new society" from working *is real incompatibility*, and the presence in a relationship of sufficient attachment to the new society to make it work so that each partner (and later their children) is better off together than they were or would be separate, regardless of differences, *is real compatibility*. Most of the clinical vignettes I am using throughout this book are instances, in my judgment, of incompatibility in this real, less inflated sense. So far as forgiveness is

[3] Turner, p. 10.

concerned, I believe the appearance of genuine incompatibility is an appropriate ground for saying "enough." When, in Turner's words, a marriage has reached the point of "irretrievable breakdown," the new society has in point of fact failed. It is, he rightly points out, not really a "ground" for *deciding* to end the marriage, but rather the recognition of an accomplished fact.[4]

FACING THE LOST CAUSE

One of the most important values in the Judaeo-Christian tradition is that of loving even when it is without return. It is exemplified in the "love your enemies" injunction with which many of us were raised, as well as by the everyday experience of acting lovingly toward people who neither know nor care that that is what we are doing —whether they be thoughtless children, mentally incompetent persons, or anonymous recipients of our work. With that value as a foundation it is frightfully hard to give up on something like a marriage. No religious tradition that I know of has found an easy way to identify and let go of a lost cause. Something keeps telling us, on either sectarian or purely secular grounds, that to be loving, forgiving people we "ought" never to give up hope and pull the plug. It is common these days for people to lament the frequency of divorce and the ease with which marriages seem to end. The frequency is undeniable, but I have serious doubts about the easy, still less cavalier, endings. My experience both as a therapist and as a divorcing person is rather the reverse: what strikes me is how *hard* it is for couples to divorce, and how some of the marriages that on appropriate grounds most clearly should be ended take forever to do so.

[4] Turner, p. 18.

I believe it is time, however, to make a sharp distinction between the unquestioned spiritual worth of loving without return, on the one hand, and the destructiveness of a clearly lost cause on the other. When we have reached the latter, we have reached the limit of forgiveness. Let me remind you of a distinction I made earlier in the chapter: the limit of forgiveness does not have to mean a feeling of crabbiness, unresolved rage, or meanness. It is more like a letting go. It is one thing for me in my heart of hearts to "forgive" someone something; it is quite another to go back for more. *That* is the limit I am talking about. That was what I meant in Chapter Three when I argued that sometimes divorce can itself be a form of reconciliation: when the destructiveness ends because two people have recognized a lost cause and refuse to go back for more mutual hurting.

I wish I had either an easy or at least a reliable way of determining when the cause is lost, but I do not. As I will be saying in more detail in the final chapter, I believe this is one of the most important functions of good marital therapy or counseling: helping a couple make as clear and responsible a determination as possible whether their marriage is in fact over. Nor am I being ingenuous about the mutuality of such a decision: many a cause is *in fact* lost when only one of the partners believes it is so. I never cease to be amazed at the extent to which a clearly wronged or abandoned ex-spouse takes upon his or her own shoulders enormous guilt and responsibility for the demise of the marriage or, perhaps worse, emotionally denies that the marriage is over even long after the decree is signed and the fact of it is clear.

Throughout this chapter we have been talking about letting go and how hard that can sometimes be, especially for people who cherish the value of forgiveness as a life principle. For those of us who experience that conflict there is a real danger of the spiritual journey of divorce coming to a screeching halt on grounds seemingly mandated by the church, or religious tradition, or the American spirit of fair play. I have tried to offer a different perspective, precisely so that the journey can continue and that one can keep on it without either sacrificing the spiritual values they hold dear or becoming paralyzed by guilt or rage. Taking a next step into the future is the topic to which we now need to turn.

NINE

Joy in the Morning: When Wishing Turns to Hope

IN OLDER DIVORCE LAW there used to be a lot of concern about "the waiting period," a required statutory time interval between, for instance, divorce and remarriage or between filing and divorce decree, depending on the law. The language has largely changed these days, but as everyone who goes through it knows, the waiting has not. I once heard it said that waiting is the most psychologically hazardous time of all, and I have no reason to doubt it. Unfortunately, the experience of divorce—before, during, and after—is riddled with waiting, and if the experience is indeed hazardous, then those of us who are divorcing spend a lot of time picking our way through an emotional mine field. At every turn of the road we have to wait. We wait for a decision to come clear whether to divorce or not; after separation we wait for agreements to be made, courts to act, and the deed to be done; after divorce we wait for some semblance of adjustment to our new life situation; and eventually we wait for new people to come into our lives, one of whom might possibly be "right."

There is no doubt it can be a toxic experience. As I write this I am "waiting" alongside a friend who discovered, to her horror, the other day that she was on the verge of throwing away a substantial amount of settlement money—far more than she could afford—just so she would not have to wait through a few more weeks of negotiation with her husband's attorneys. Many an unwise remarriage has taken place for no more compelling reason than that someone got tired of waiting. More than once in my divorcing experience I mentally laid these two biblical sentiments side by side and tried, unsuccessfully, to get them married: "Wait, I say, on the Lord," and "How long, O Lord, how long?" There was not much doubt which one spoke more eloquently for me!

I am certain that waiting is an inevitable and unpleasant part of divorcing; I do not believe, however, that it *has* to be destructive, and introducing you to that notion—and a way of making the difference—is the aim of this chapter. To put it succinctly, there is one kind of waiting that is negative, whose fruits are denial and self-pity. It culminates in a life of unproductive wishing. But there is another kind of waiting that even in its pain produces growth. It leads to a life of hope. Between those two lies a world of difference, the difference between divorce as a spiritual journey and divorce as tumbling backward through a tunnel of failure, recrimination, and unreality.

To begin to discern the difference, we must start with a plain but startlingly often forgotten fact: divorce is inescapably an experience of *grief.* I am simply amazed at the number of well-educated and intelligent divorcing people who fail either to realize or to acknowledge the importance of the fact that they are going through a time of mourning or grieving whose inner dynamics are no different from what they would be experiencing at the death of a person significant to them. To be honest, I am amazed at how often during the divorcing process I myself, whose business it is to deal with these things, forgot it.

But grief it certainly is, for the simple reason that grieving is the natural human response to *any* loss, and divorce is an experience of multiple loss of the highest order: the loss of a spouse, loss of a family pattern, loss of a dream about what marriage would be, loss of home, loss of economic status, loss of friends, and—difficult though it may be to admit—loss of all those negative patterns of interaction with a spouse that part of us is glad to be free from but another part had undeniably come to expect as a familiar emotional landscape—the "devil" we at least knew.

Psychologists and others have only been studying grief for a short time—less than fifty years, really—but we know some reliable things about it. (I would suggest, for instance, that any divorcing person read any of several excellent books on grief, even though their focus may be on loss through death.) We cannot begin to summarize everything here, but there are some important high points to note. We know, as I have just said, that grief happens to some extent whenever we lose something, whether it is a person through death, or a job or a house or, for that matter, a favorite old hat. We know that people "learn" how to grieve over the years through successions of relatively manageable loss experiences that "teach" them in an emotional sense how to incorporate into their lives the later experience of losing even bigger and more important things. The small child whose pet mouse dies is having an experience that is directly tied to what she will go through when a parent or a spouse dies. People who for some reason have *not* had enough such manageable loss experiences growing up, or who have not been adequately nurtured through them, are particularly vulnerable to devastation when a major loss experience finally does come along—as inevitably it must.

We know, too, that there is a certain shape and pattern to the grief experience, even though I would caution anyone against woodenly adopting any set of "stages of grief" as the absolute truth. There is an evolution of feeling from initial nonacceptance and resistance, through a time of inner pain and emptiness, to a point of getting on with life again. Familiar feelings along the way are anger, sadness, panic, guilt, and eventually relief, hopefulness, and joy— "Weeping may stay for the night, but joy comes in the morning," as the Bible has it in that line of a psalm beloved of religious and nonreligious people alike (Ps. 30:5).

An image I often use with grieving people to describe what is happening to them emotionally is that of a ship leaving port. Two things must happen: one by one the lines attaching it to the shore must be cast off, one at a time, until it is free to sail; and then its inertia and resistance must be gradually overcome as it gains way. Then in due time it will reattach in another port. So, too, with human beings: one by one we set aside the connections to what we have lost, so that in time we will be able to make them anew, elsewhere, and slowly and painfully we get moving.

That grieving is a response to loss is certain; *how we conduct our grieving*, however, is something in which we have some room for choice and influence, sometimes with a helping hand along the way, and that is what this brief discussion of the subject has been leading up to. Essentially we can choose either to embrace the process as one of growth, no matter how painful, or we can try to dodge it or make it go away. All of us, I daresay, flirt with the second to some degree, even if we know intellectually (which is true) that grief cannot really be avoided. It can be delayed, or derailed, or diverted, but at the end of the day its influence, perhaps now camouflaged and made even more troublesome, will be there. *What I am saying in this chapter is that whether our waiting experience in divorce is creative or poisonous depends in large measure on how we handle our grief.*

A moment ago I said that divorcing people sometimes do not recognize their experience as one of grief. That needs a little more elaboration at this point, and two examples come to mind to explain why. The first is a church group of divorcing people I spoke to not long ago, comprised of about a dozen very diverse people with equally varied experiences—a young woman married less than two years, a man old enough to be her father whose wife had left him after the kids were grown, a jocular businessman openly on the hunt for a new mate, an obviously competent middle-aged career woman in her second divorce, and so on. Some were cheerful, others morose; some had initiated their divorce, while others had not wanted it at all; some were verbal and open, others tightly shut down and uncommunicative. What struck me, however, was that despite their differences in situation, way of responding to it, and conscious feeling, *all of them were in the psychological process of grieving for their losses, whether they recognized it or not.*

The moral to the story is that grief or mourning is an internal experience involving the whole process of personal organization rather than a particular conscious "feeling." Some of those people were surprised to hear me say that they were "grieving." "Hell no," one would have said, "I was never so relieved in my life as getting out of that marriage." Another would have said she was so furiously angry at the way her husband had treated and left her that there were no bereaved feelings at all. Still another would have shrugged his shoulders and said, "Hey, it happened and it's over and I'm giving all my attention now to the dating I never did before I got married." Their experiences and their feelings were very different and sometimes did not look at all like the popular image of typical grieving—the sadness, the missing, the yearning, the aimlessness. But in terms of the internal process of detaching from something once strongly held, positively or negatively, which is what mourning fundamentally is, *all* were experiencing grief.

I look back on my own experience in that respect with some chagrin, given my profession. I was aware of my grief in some areas, but not in all of them. I knew the sense of loss connected with a home I had loved and poured a lot of energy into, and I felt acutely the loss of an intact family, as well as the loss of a long-held and tended dream of what marriage might be; but curiously I felt no conscious grief about the marital relationship per se. I told myself that must be because my wife and I had done a thorough and, I believe, conscientious job of marriage counseling, working through issues and feelings, and finally accepting what on balance there was no realistic alternative to. I was wrong. When a bit later a new friendship with a woman who was really not much more than a recent acquaintance turned sour, I hit the emotional mat like a bag of cement. Slowly—and with help—I came to see that my grief about the marriage had been there unacknowledged all along, but that the conscious *feeling* of loss and devastation appeared only indirectly in connection with yet another loss experience that, emotionally speaking, just was not strong enough in and of itself to have caused that degree of intense reaction. Everyone is different, of course, but in my own case I learned to "read" my experiences and find what *for me* were telltale signs of grieving in ways I thought about and reacted to a variety of things. When the signs appeared, I knew that, regardless what my actual current feelings about the lost marriage were at the moment, that was the real issue and I had better connect with it.

That leads to my second example. Years ago my friend and colleague Dr. Robert E. Buxbaum and I conducted a therapy group for divorced women in the church I then served as pastor. The lengths of time since these women had been divorced ranged from fifteen years to two months, with most of them several years away from the experience and outwardly pretty well recovered from it. As the life of the group unfolded, however, a curious and heartbreaking thing came to light: *none* of them was "divorced" in an emotional sense. To one degree or another all of them were still attached to their ex-spouses and their former marriages because the grieving process had gone unrecognized and was incomplete. "Complete," of course is a tricky word, and just as I am arguing that divorcing is an extended process rather than a single event, so, too, grieving is not something about which a person easily can one day say, "There, that's over and done with." I will be coming back to that aspect of things in a few minutes. We can nevertheless identify the ways in which that process is moving along appropriately toward a resolution (the result of which is that a person is ready and able to reinvest the psychic energy that formerly had been bound up with the loss experience) or the ways in which it has gotten stalled or derailed. This group of women was a vivid example of the kind of lingering hurt and incapacitation that can happen when grieving is not done. I look back on myself and realize with trepidation how close I came to joining them.

The point of all this is really to say (especially to those of you who would not immediately locate yourselves in an experience of grief as a result of divorce) that though it takes many forms and though one's conscious feeling may not *seem* like what we usually think of as grieving, the divorcing experience inescapably involves mourning because it always involves loss. The question is not *whether* you will grieve, but *how.* That having been said, we can now return to the main subject of this chapter, the two ways of waiting.

For people in a waiting position one of the most important distinctions that can be made, on both theological and psychological grounds, is between *wishing* and *hoping.* In everyday speech we sometimes use those terms interchangeably. It would be better and more accurate if we did not, because when it comes to the actual experience, the difference is crucial. Wishing is something we learn as children and it partakes of magic—wishing on a star, waiting for the genie in the bottle, pulling the wishbone at Thanksgiving. The magic is essential to the fun, and childhood would not be the same without it. It gives us, among other things, the capacity to dream and to reach. Gradually, however, a child comes to learn something else: that while wishing makes for great fairy tales, in the real world it takes a boost from human initiative to bring it off with any reliability. Now something distinctly unmagical but nevertheless marvelous has happened. The excitement and energizing power of the wish team up with a sense of being able to make a difference in one's life so that we do not have to live with our fingers crossed, at the mercy of some unknown force of good or bad luck. One can work to make things happen the way one wants. The results will not always be just what we had in mind, of course, but the process works often enough to give the child, and soon the adult, a sense of autonomy, initiative, and competence. As that developmental process unfolds, something crucial takes the place of wishing: *hope.*

Wishing is, after all, inherently a capricious business; even the tooth fairy is not 100 percent reliable by the time you get to twelve-year molars. But if wishing is based in the magical thinking appropriate to young childhood, hoping is based in reality, in the experience of at least enough good things happening the way one envisioned, worked for, and perhaps trusted others, including a transcendent Other, to help with. As an adult I therefore learn to notice the difference between the *wishing* I will still playfully do from time to time, realizing all the while that it is a form of magical thinking based in fantasy, and the *hoping* that grows out of realistically wanting something and doing what I can to bring it about, perhaps putting my want in the spiritual perspective of forces at work in the universe far beyond my control or understanding, whether I call it God or fate or destiny. When what I hope for is delayed or does not materialize or turns out opposite from my original vision, I can deal with the disappointment on some grounds *other* than chance, bad luck, or not wishing hard enough. Even if, in religious terms, I conclude that God did not intend or permit things to go as I had hoped, I can still often enough find real reasons for the outcome, whether I like them or not. I may be bitterly disappointed, baffled, or furious, but I will not in the main believe myself to be utterly in the hands of random ill fortune—and therefore helpless.

Probably nothing so taxes my capacity to hope as the experience of major loss and its attendant grief. In the waiting time of grief I become particularly vulnerable to two enemies of the human spirit, self-pity and wishful thinking. Both are psychological realities to be reckoned with, and both can cost me the hope without which life eventually is not worth living. What I am arguing here is that we ourselves have a fundamental say in the matter of which way our life goes, as spiritual journey or depressive dead end. Let me describe the options in the form of two different people and their reactions, each a composite of what I am trying to describe.

Each person has experienced a painful divorce and the psychic dislocation it almost always brings to one degree or another. Each is now in a waiting time, no matter where they are in the divorcing process, waiting at the very least for life to regain some semblance of equilibrium, even if "normalcy" is too distant—or painful—a possibility to envision. Each is experiencing grief, though there the similarity ends.

Our first person adopts as a basic emotional posture that he or she is a *victim*—of an ex-spouse's chicanery, limitation, or bad faith, a victim of fate, of bad luck, of betrayal, of anything in the world that offers itself as a plausible explanation. The main thing is that this person's response to the undeniable loss he or she has suffered is a self-picture that is victimized, "done unto." Our person's feeling about him- or herself is aptly described by the term "self-pitying." The inner message that plays endlessly like a phone off the hook is "poor me." The person experiences sadness, perhaps actual depression, immobilization, and a sense of helplessness. Things will be right, if they ever will, only if someone "out there" does something for me— and even that may be more than my self-pity has room to contemplate. All the self-pitying person can do is *wish*, as a child might, for things to be better, or perhaps for them never to have gone sour in the first place. One is as realistic as the other, because for this person there is no *energy* in the wishing, and it stands little chance of accomplishing anything except recycling the self-pity when the wish does not come true. Even if such a person's circumstance is indeed dire and much to be pitied, it is important to realize that a form of denial is strongly at work in the reaction. Perhaps it is a denial of some actual facts of matters—their own role and responsibility in the divorce, or the inevitability of ending an impossible marriage, or the possibility that things could ever get better and they might live and love again. On the outside it may *look* like such a person is facing the awful truth and grieving. Inside, however, nothing could be further from the truth. The "poor me" syndrome is not about the business of detaching from what has been lost, no matter how painfully, *but rather is unconsciously concerned with staying emotionally attached in a way that both denies the reality of the loss and perpetuates the self-pity that is a substitute for real grieving.* Interestingly, there is growing evidence that the self-pity that comes from adopting a posture of victimization actually has a brain-chemical effect in the release of pain-killing endorphins and is therefore *literally* "addictive."[1]

Even ordinary observation will quickly tell you, however, that the wishful thinking of people lost in the "poor me's" is something of a sham: if the tooth fairy somehow *did* materialize to grant their wishes, one has the feeling that the last thing they would do is take it. For this person waiting is agony, a time full of denial, self-pity, and wishful unreality. No matter how mournful they appear, and I assure you it can be heart-wrenching to be with them, they are not grieving and they are not growing. Mention "hope" to them and you will get an abrupt dismissal of such a notion as impossible if not downright cruel. The sad thing is that so long as the downward spiral of self-pity and denial continues, they are right.

Our second person is not, let me say at the beginning, a psychological or spiritual hero or heroine. He or she has not leaped any tall emotional buildings in a single bound lately and may be visibly moving no faster than the steam locomotive in your local museum. But, unlike with our first person, something very important is happening: *they have chosen, consciously or unconsciously, to live the role of someone who is recovering from the loss of something important, with the whole panoply of feelings that involves, rather than the role of a victim.* Crisis workers at the scene of natural disasters

---

[1] I am indebted to my psychiatrist colleague Dr. Henry W. Ratliffe for his insight and research into this phenomenon.

can spot the difference almost at once: after the initial shock has passed, some people begin the slow process of putting their lives back together even through tears and heartbreak, while some sit lost in their miasma. The difference comes from the way they "frame" and interpret what has happened to them, *not* in any difference in the basic pain of loss they feel. Our second person has begun to grieve, that is, to cast off the lines that had moored him or her to the dock being left behind—the spouse, the home, the family life, the dream of marriage, and yes, even the fights and bitterness. This person does not for a minute *like* his or her grief, but nevertheless embraces it, seeks to understand how it operates, lets it do its slow, healing work. If such a person has indeed been wronged, treated unjustly or brutally, suffered the slings and arrows of outrageous fortune, then for them that is something to be recognized, to be angry about, and perhaps to seek appropriate compensation for. But that is very different from taking the role of victim, from coming to see oneself as *defined by* having been hurt. That may be the clearest I can be about it: the self-pitying person has, in effect, taken on board a new self-definition, that of victim, whereas the grieving second person has suffered an experience from which he or she seeks to recover.

I am not saying for a minute, by the way, that the waiting our second person experiences is going to be a jolly time. It will in fact be a time of moving back and forth between hope and despair, the difference perhaps being that one knows it is indeed a movement back and forth, rather like a boat one knows and trusts enough in its rolling in heavy seas to realize it will not, after all, go all the way over—no matter that you are hanging on to the rail for dear life or hunkered down in nauseous fear in the bottom of its cabin. It is just this dialectic between hope and despair in fact that, to me, is a sign of recovery and journey. I worry, as is obvious, about the self-pitying victim, and I worry about the too cheerful denier of all that has happened, precisely because for both these kinds of people that dialectic has been collapsed and denied, and what has been lost is the opportunity for real hope.

What, then, could we say spells the difference between these two kinds of people—let us call them the "victim" and the "recoverer"—and the two kinds of waiting, between wishful thinking and realistic hope? More or less without trying we have already formulated a kind of checklist, which I would summarize as follows:

1. The recoverer treats his or her experience of loss in divorce *as an experience* to be lived out, understood, and made a part of personal history; the victim allows that experience to impart a whole new role in life, that of a person who has been victimized.

2. The recoverer lives out a full range of emotional reactions, including sadness, anger, relief, fear, and joy; the victim narrows his or her emotional life into a band of basic self-pity.

3. The recoverer gets about the emotional business of detaching from what has been lost; the victim stays attached by dwelling on how he or she has suffered.

4. The recoverer accepts swings of attitude and feeling between hope and despair and works toward creating a different future; the victim tries to relieve his or her negative feelings with wishing things were different in the here-and-now—or worse, in the past.

5. The recoverer seeks to understand in as much detail as possible what he or she has experienced and why; the victim tries to close off the experience itself *either* by refusing to think about it *or* by dwelling on the hurt that has been suffered.

6. For the recoverer waiting has the character of *waiting for* something to develop, even if he or she cannot describe very well just what it is beyond a basic feeling of

"better than now"; for the victim waiting is a sterile experience of getting through one more day, with more of the same ahead.

7. The recoverer hopes; the victim wishes.
8. The recoverer takes steps to connect his or her life with other people and their needs; the victim resists involvement with other people and events in order to turn inward to his or her feelings of being done badly by.

I am aware that in describing the waiting time by using these two composite images I risk giving a kind of "either/or" impression that is not really accurate. Each of us in fact experiences both kinds of waiting and their attendant feelings and experiences to one degree or another. The question is more what one's dominant perspective and outlook is, what one is *most* of the time, even if occasionally we veer over to the other side. Let me also make clear that in describing the "recoverer's" kind of waiting I am not talking about "positive thinking," turning our backs on negativity, pulling ourselves up by our own bootstraps, or any such slick thing. It is a different *inner orientation* I am trying to describe, intellectually, emotionally, and spiritually, rather than a difference in inner strength, positive outlook, happy feelings, or carefreeness. We cannot choose what we feel, as the positive thinkers seem to want to say; but we do have some power of choice in the basic posture we adopt in response to those feelings. The evidence is strong that people can learn to recognize the onset of self-pity and set it aside in favor of more genuine grieving.

In all literature, both religious and secular, there is probably no more graphic or moving example of this hopeful kind of waiting than in certain of the Psalms in the Bible that are known collectively as the "Psalms of Lament," perhaps as much as a third of the entire Book of

Psalms.[2] Here is poetry written from the absolute depths. Here is what theologian Martin Marty calls a "wintry kind of faith" that gives utterance to a "cry of absence."[3] Here is the psalmist shaking a fist in the face of a God who seems to have gone clean off the stage and left us to ruin. But here, in the very angry, desperate address to an absent God, in the audaciousness of lifting a prayer when, as far as the psalmist can see, the evidence is completely damning, is the voice of hope and the unmistakable sound of footfalls on a spiritual journey.

[2] See especially Psalms 3, 5, 13, 17, 22, 25, 26, 27, 31, 35, 38, 39, 42, 51, 55, 57, 59, 77, 88, 123, 140, 141, 142, 143.

[3] Martin E. Marty, *A Cry of Absence: Reflections for the Winter of the Heart* (San Francisco: Harper & Row, Publishers, 1983).

TEN

The Return of the Self

COMMITTEE MEETINGS are not typically occasions of great personal discovery, but for reasons known but to God it was while sitting through one some months after my divorce that I found out something about myself whose importance rings as true today as it did then. I remember thinking on two levels at the same time, both paying attention to the business at hand and ruminating about my divorce (as divorcing people seem to do—a lot). I have no idea what combination of conscious agenda and unconscious imagery produced the thought that was about to happen, but suddenly, sitting straighter in my seat, the light went on! I said inside, *"I've got my self back!"* It was a thunderously simple thought that would take me much longer to decipher the meaning of, but it hit me like a ton of bricks. Somehow I had gotten back (without fully realizing how much I had even lost it) some identifiable, almost touchable sense of being a self, and the only way to describe that experience is, in my teenage sons' language, "awesome."

Since then I have discovered that a similar experience is not uncommon with divorcing people, though usually it does not get put into words. Perhaps for that reason it sometimes goes unnoticed. It can be one of those high moments of integration and freedom even amidst the wreckage of divorce, and as I have thought about it since, I believe that it points to some terribly important and often neglected aspects of the spiritual journey of divorce. "The return of the self" is what this chapter is about.

Immediately, of course, a slightly negative cant, a mildly shameful hue adheres to the subject. Most of us are taught from a very early age, on either religious or general ethical grounds, that the idea of "self" combines with certain things to produce distinctly negative results. We are trained to be on guard against becoming self*ish*, self-*absorbed*, self-*centered*, self-*conscious*, self-*deceived*, self-*important*, self-*pitying*, self-*serving*, self-*righteous*, and on and on. By contrast, the positive shopping list for the self is much shorter, including the virtues of being self-*less*, self-*giving*, and self-*sacrificing*, and also adding (though often with some cautiousness) being self-*confident*, self-*controlled*, self-*possessed*, self-*reliant*, and self-*respectful*. Clearly the self is a ready instrument of abuse if we do not watch out. The very idea of taking care of one's "self," of valuing it and protecting it and—taking the Golden Rule at face value—*loving* it is fraught with peril. A novelist like Ayn Rand can write on "The Virtue of Selfishness," but even after we discover what she means, the very title itself sounds like a contradiction in terms.

When we get married our selves are joined with other selves ("two becoming one" or some similar language traditionally marking the event) and the virtues of the self listed above reach what poets, theologians, and ordinary folks traditionally believe is their finest hour. Giving of oneself in a marriage, bearing each other's burdens, and serving rather than being served are the common coin of marital value and stability. I want to be clearly on record as affirming that absolutely. But I also want to explore how that process can go awry in marriage, and how if we are not careful it can distort and corrode our experience of divorce, leaving us hobbled by a dying relationship rather than freed for a new and better life.

We have already talked about how in the process of grieving over a loss we reclaim the energy, investment, and parts of ourselves that had been attached to the lost person or object. Something related to that is what I mean by "getting oneself back" after divorce. It is both necessary and terribly difficult. My basic idea here is that accomplishing it requires that we understand very clearly the role of the self in marriage and perhaps then correct our misunderstanding of it. *I believe that what it means to give of oneself, bear another's burdens, and serve the other in marriage are often badly distorted and that this distortion can bring the journey of divorce to a screeching halt if we do not change it.* That is our business now.

GIVING ONESELF IN MARRIAGE

In the traditional language of the wedding service the bride is "given" to be married (though increasing numbers of women quite appropriately object to being talked about in such object-like terms). Actually, something far more pervasive is going on, as both partners "give themselves" to this "new society," the marriage. By that we usually mean several kinds of things: a willingness to give up some measure of our own comfort, independence, and control; a capacity to hold our partner's needs, desires, and values in as high esteem as our own (which is the psychiatrist Harry Stack Sullivan's very definition of "love"[1]); a sharing of our histories, experiences (negative and positive), and dreams with those of the other; and a commitment to spend our energy and substance freely for the common cause of the marriage. The list could go on, of course, but that is enough to illustrate the basic process at work in "self-giving."

What, you might ask, could possibly go wrong with that or be misunderstood about it? Two things commonly do, in my experience. In the first place, notice that I have used the language of giving oneself *to the marriage* rather than *to the partner* (in the same way that the "giving of the bride" is *not* to the husband but rather "to be married"). That is a subtle, but I believe important, distinction in the way we perceive ourselves in the process. Particularly in the first blush of love we, of course, do not think of it that way at all. We think and often talk about giving ourselves to our spouses, about doing and being things *for them.* Is not that, after all, the very bedrock of the loving relationship? Increasingly I do not believe so. For one thing, I do not know how—literally—I could receive another's giving of herself to me. What would that entail? What would I do with it? And for another, if my partner has given herself to me, what has happened to *her?* All those things we just listed above as being involved in the exchange, are they no longer hers as well? No, I suggest that something very

---

[1] Harry Stack Sullivan, *The Interpersonal Theory of Psychiatry* (New York: W. W. Norton & Company, Inc., 1953) p. 245. A state of love for another person exists, says Sullivan, when to us that person is of equal importance in all fields of value.

different is (or should be) happening: we give of ourselves to the marriage, to the new society of which we both are the members. We pour ourselves into the same well, from which we both drink.

Without that distinction something damaging happens to our own autonomy and selfhood, with the paradoxical result that in the end we have nothing left of ourselves to give, day in and day out. It is the shared commitment to the marriage, this new creation, that joins us. Our being for each other is, so to speak, indirect, mediated by the marriage that now "holds" us, in both spiritual and psychological terms. Two prominent marital therapists, David and Jill Scharff have observed that one test question for a healthy marriage is whether the relationship itself is capable of "holding" its members, particularly in times of need and stress.[2] Let me offer a personal example of how it works. Not long before this writing my fiancee and I hit a serious snag of pain and disagreement, which I have to confess was 100 percent my own creation and responsibility. Details are not important; the point is that I had unintentionally but thoughtlessly put her in a very uncomfortable and untenable position that hurt her badly. What hurt the most in fact was that because I was so engrossed in my own feelings at the time, I did not see it coming and anticipate how it would feel for her. Where now could she turn for understanding and consolation? To me, her partner? Yes and no. Yes, she did make it clear to me what she was feeling and I saw my error and felt incredibly bad about it. But I, after all, was also the perpetrator and nothing could change that. Thinking of giving myself—in this

---

[2] David E. and Jill Savege Scharff, *Object Relations Family Therapy* (Northvale, N.J.: Jason Aronson, Inc., 1985) p. 62. Their use of the metaphor of "holding" is exactly that of D. W. Winnicott, whose ideas we will use in Chapter Eleven. It is a profoundly important concept that comes from the basic experience of a mother's holding her child and providing it with the boundary and protection it needs to face the daunting prospect of becoming a member of the outer world.

case, my flawedness and my remorse—to her was small comfort, if it could be done at all. Though we talked at length and held each other achingly, she really turned not so much to me *but to our relationship* for what she needed, and found it. Something about our love, about the new society we are in process of creating, allowed this experience of personal betrayal to be different from others, so that we both could be held and comforted not so much by each other as by what we had jointly created. In a literal sense, of course, she turned to me as well, but mainly insofar as I am the other member of that relationship. The relationship to which we have both given ourselves is what held both of us and joined us in this crisis; we drank from the well we had both filled. Mind you, we did not talk it out in this way at the time; but a telltale bit of evidence that what I have described was in fact what was happening was her spontaneous comment as we passed the flash point of crisis and entered the aftermath of pain, "You know, I have never felt more married to you than I did today." Sometimes, then, it is not *what we give* that poses the problem but rather what we give it *to*. I am convinced that if my fiancee and I had, in effect, given ourselves to each other rather than to our relationship, we could not have gotten through that crisis the way we did, with, in the end, pardon, new commitment, and healing.

The other thing that goes wrong with self-giving seems to follow from our habit of construing the gift as being to the partner rather than to the relationship. Sometimes we think of it—and actually use the term—as "surrender." We surrender to a person, not to a relationship. It is strange that people use the idea of self-surrender as something noble and positive when every ordinary connotation of that term is negative. I believe it should be in this case, too. Surrendering something means I lose it because something more powerful than I has, in effect, taken it away from me. If in a relationship we think of surrendering ourselves, it tends to become an emptying out process, a loss rather than a giving, and the two are very different.

Two examples will illustrate the contrast. Martha was a bright and enormously talented middle-aged woman who came through a difficult divorce badly bruised but far wiser than before. Her concept of giving herself had been framed entirely in terms of "surrendering" herself to her husband for the sake of the marriage, and he in turn was a man who could not tolerate his wife's having competencies or achievements that matched, still worse exceeded, some of his own. Over the years Martha had curtailed her interests, activities, and career, limiting herself to home-making and child-rearing. When the marriage finally ended, she began slowly to reclaim some of what she had given up, and discovered, in the way I described in opening this chapter, that she was a person of substance and talent whom she liked and wanted to claim as a self she had lost during her married years. For her marriage she had tried to change herself to match the wishes and expectations of her husband; thinking of it as a giving of herself to him meant, of course, taking into account what was acceptable to him and "surrendering" herself as a consequence. After it was over, she was able to say in healthy anger, "I will never ever surrender myself for another person again. Adapt, learn, modify, yes, all those things, but I will never again change myself to fit what I think someone wants me to be, not in extreme and not in total." She had learned the critical difference between self-giving and surrender.

Another example was offered by a counseling client, Lynn, in a different context from divorce. Lynn had become paralyzed as the result of an accident and was having a difficult time making the adjustment from a formerly active physical life to confinement in a wheelchair. Her minister talked to her about the importance, in religious terms, of "surrender," of giving oneself up to the situation rather than fighting it. But "fight" it is precisely what she wanted—and needed—to do, not in the sense of denying her current reality but rather in coming to make the best possible use of herself in a radically changed and tragic situation. *Accepting* her reality and "surrendering," as her minister had well-meaningly but inaccurately advised, were very different things. Perhaps the crucial ingredient in both these examples is the matter of *using* oneself appropriately: you cannot use what you have surrendered; it is no longer there to give and keep on giving. "Surrender" is indeed a term that has positive currency in some religious circles. Carefully used, it is intended to mean giving up willfulness or pridefulness or arrogance in order that God's purposes for a person might become known and fulfilled. It is the sort of thing meant in the Apostle Paul's conversion experience when he hears a voice from heaven saying, "Saul, Saul, why do you persecute me? It hurts you to kick against the goads" (Acts 26:14). "Surrender" properly means not a loss of self but a giving over of the self to be used in a better way. So far, so good, but unfortunately, and perhaps because of the ordinary connotations of the word, "surrender" in either religious or marital usage has too easily meant emptying oneself into passivity and becoming either a doormat or a lapdog—both of which have their places, but not in either marriage or religious experience.

Thus far I have talked almost entirely about marriage. What, one might well be asking, does this have to do with the return of the self in divorce? Basically what I am suggesting is that getting one's self back from a failed marriage is far more difficult if we have fallen into the distortions just discussed of what giving oneself means. If I have indeed framed or conceived of the process as one of surrendering myself to another person, rather than giving of myself to a relationship, then I may have a very difficult time reversing the process. For one thing, "surrendering" means losing, and if I have spent years persuading myself that certain of my qualities, attributes, abilities, or characteristics needed to be set aside rather than used (and in the process perhaps modified), then I have some major relearning and rediscovering to do *about myself.* And for another, if I have thought of the whole process as directed toward a partner rather than a marriage, I am liable to get stuck on the simple fact that while the marriage no longer exists the other person *does.* Getting myself back, then, is more apt to seem like larceny than recovery. Again and again I encounter divorcing people who still carry an unrealistic picture of their obligations toward an ex-spouse, whether it is because they are caught by the "friendly divorce" myth we discussed in Chapter Two or because they feel they "owe" some things to a person they spent conceivably many married years with. That sense of owing, I suspect, comes just from this distorted way of having looked at the self-giving of marriage. By contrast, when I begin to think of it in terms of the relationship rather than the partner, I can begin to say something like this to myself: "I gave as much of myself as I could to a marriage, and for whatever reason it did not work. Now that relationship does not exist and has no claim on me. My children and family certainly do have a claim on me, but my marriage does not and my former spouse does not beyond what we have legally agreed to. I will try to treat him or her as civilly and as decently as I would any other person, but what I gave of myself to the marriage, the marriage in its demise now gives back to me, *and it is taking nothing from my former partner for it to do so.* What I gave it, it has now returned, for me to do with as I choose." Then, I believe, is when one finds oneself sitting in a dreary committee meeting, jerked bolt upright by the realization that my once given "self," bruised and perhaps half-forgotten, is back.

BEARING EACH OTHER'S BURDENS

Selfishness in marriage is as destructive and unlovable as it is anywhere else, *if* by it we mean indifference to the needs and interests of others whom we are otherwise committed to paying attention to.[3] But "selfishness" in the very different sense of respecting our needs and wants precisely so we are able to "expand to embrace the well-being of our partner" so that "his or her happiness is of *selfish* importance to ourselves" is a very different matter.[4] It is, as Branden passionately argues, of the essence of love. Looking back over my experience as a therapist I make this startling discovery: of all the many people who worried about whether they were being selfish in a relationship, none in fact was. The genuinely selfish ones—in the more traditional, negative sense—were those who never mentioned it, indeed perhaps could not even perceive it. It is the overt worriers who, in turn, worry me, because they are concerned about a dominant spiritual value, and when it comes to divorce, too often they are not getting the help and clarification they deserve.

Many of these people have committed themselves on either specifically religious or generally humanitarian grounds to the value of what is often called "bearing one another's burdens" in relationships. When the time comes that they either cannot or choose not to continue doing so, they are faced with the agonizing question, "Am I being selfish?" Am I going against the grain of what was taught me as a Jewish or Christian or plain humanitarian ethic, that, particularly in something like marriage or an inti-

[3] Nathaniel Branden, *The Psychology of Romantic Love* (New York: Bantam Books, 1980) p. 169. Branden's whole discussion of "selfishness" and its importance for love is thought-provoking and helpful.

[4] Branden, pp. 169–70.

mate relationship, sharing my partner's burdens, struggles, issues, and trials is one of the highest forms of love, moral behavior, or downright spiritual obligation? That question may be most acute early in the divorcing process, when a person is trying to decide whether to end a marriage or not, and part of the agonizing has to do with determining what I owe to whom on moral or spiritual grounds. But whether it is then or later in the divorcing process when one looks back and tries to take responsibility for what happened, the business of bearing each other's burdens may rise up to stop us dead in our tracks: if we were *really* doing that, would we be thinking of or would we have done something so "selfish" as getting out?

Here, as was true with the question of self-giving, a lot depends on making a careful distinction about the way we think about, talk about, and actually do the business of our interaction with a person. *It is one thing to try to share or bear one another's burdens; it is something else again to take over another's responsibility.* The former, though found explicitly in the New Testament (Gal. 6:2), has the approval in one form or another of all major religious and ethical value systems. The latter is a formula for trouble in a marriage, unnecessary guilt in a divorce, and major difficulties in any kind of relationship. All too often people are bothered because they think they have failed at the first, when in fact they are healthily and appropriately getting free of the second, as they should. Or to put it differently, what "bearing each other's burdens" means is *not at all the same as* taking over each other's responsibilities. Let us look at the differences first in terms of the burden-bearing idea and its biblical source, and second in terms of responsibility-meddling and what family therapists call "triangulation."

The injunction to "Bear one another's burdens and so fulfill the law of Christ" (Gal. 6:2) has over the centuries, like many such popular biblical verses, been lifted out of context and generalized far beyond what it originally meant. That may not be all bad, but we owe it to ourselves at least to *know* what the more exact intention of the saying is. The line occurs in an argument the Apostle Paul is making to the Christians in the church at Galatia, trying to get them to ease up on their condemning attitudes toward those who sin and do wrong. He says quite plainly that if you find someone caught in any wrongdoing, the thing to do is "restore" that person in a gentle way, taking into due account that you, too, are not free from the same kind of misbehavior. Then occurs the line, "Bear one another's burdens," referring precisely to the matter of not ostracizing a wrongdoer in the conceited and mistaken belief that you yourself are exempt. Curiously, the argument ends a few lines later with a completely paradoxical verse, which unfortunately is *not* remembered and quoted: "For each person will have to bear his or her own load"! The meaning of the paradox is clear enough: because you are aware of having your own "load" of error and wrongdoing to shoulder, you should be willing to bear with the similar load of other people and not start pointing fingers or throwing religious daggers. *The fundamental meaning of "bearing one another's burdens" therefore is a warning against self-righteousness and religious or legal arrogance in the face of wrongdoing or error.* It is not a general prescription for helping other people with their life's problems and issues. That latter may indeed be a good thing, but you cannot get it out of this particular text.

Now that meaning would seem to have a ready application in the human relationship of marriage and equally of divorce. It would say, in effect, that when a partner is in the wrong, self-righteous blaming is inappropriate because we, too, are very likely to have the same kind of behavior to account for in some other respect. No one is perfect. The better way is to seek to help the wrongdoer mend his or her ways and absorb the natural consequences of whatever it is that has happened.

I am not necessarily trying to persuade you to narrow the application of the burden-bearing idea back to its original context. Even if we let it expand beyond wrongdoing to more general life issues, as popular usage has done, the underlying meaning is sharply different from something like tending other people's business. It still has to do with the basic awareness that because I, too, have my life issues to deal with, the appropriate stance to take toward the other person is one of empathy and cooperation—even in the midst of necessary confrontation and consequences. Self-righteousness is ruled out: that is the main force of the idea, whether in its narrow biblical or broader popular use. If I am to "use" myself in such a situation it will be by understanding and communicating that I, too, experience and perhaps suffer from the same kinds of life issues, limitations, errors, and challenges. I am therefore able to offer a person the same kind of support, forgiveness, or fellow-traveling I will surely want to have when the wheel spins and it is my turn to need it. I see no reason why an appropriately "nonfriendly" version of that sort of posture and self-giving cannot be had in the civility of a responsible divorce, just as it can in a good marriage, though plain human reality says it is more difficult when you would just as happily see your ex-spouse "neighbor" go over a cliff.

The bottom line, then, is that if a person wants to embody and act on the spiritual value contained in the idea of bearing one another's burdens, one does so by keeping free of self-righteousness and blind denunciation. What was never intended was that we should take over the other person's task or issue and make it our own; yet it is something like that understanding that often delays or prevents the "return of the self" in divorce. Let us take a look at how it operates.

If you wanted a one-sentence statement of what students and therapists of the family believe is the master key to understanding what troubles family (and marital) relationships, I think it would be something like this: *Anytime a person tries to do someone else's work for them, there's going to be trouble.* A more colorful version of the same idea that I happen to like is the (supposedly) ancient Chinese saying, "Why do you hate me? I never did anything to help you." Again and again in relationships people either knowingly or unknowingly, willingly or by conscription, fall into the trap of trying to do someone else's work—by which I mean such things as fulfill their roles, express their feelings, absorb their worries, make up for their failings, complete their tasks, conduct their relationships, take up their responsibilities, and anything else that would come under the category of tending another person's emotional, relational, and situational onions.

To make matters even more complicated, this displacement of responsibility goes on both intergenerationally and unconsciously, so that it is not at all unusual for people today to be "doing the work" of a family member from a previous generation, perhaps as their immediate predecessor in the family tree had done, all with no conscious knowledge of what is happening—except that typically something is sour in the family system and needs help. My aim here is not to talk generally about family dynamics but rather to lay the groundwork for looking at this third aspect of what hinders the return of the self in divorce.

As you have already read, my basic idea is that we have misunderstood and overdone the basic desire to help other people by "bearing their burdens." We all too often take that to mean that we should shoulder part or all of their own responsibilities, and when that happens we have entered the danger zone of relational dysfunction just described. The reason that is so troublesome will already be familiar to you from previous pages: when we take over someone else's responsibility, we violate their boundaries and impede their taking up their own roles in whatever area is at issue. Paradoxically, in an effort to be "helpful" in this way we insure a person's failure—failure to do whatever it is they need to do and grow from the results, even if they are painful or negative. Family therapist Edwin Friedman has coined a marvelous term for it: "overfunctioning in someone else's space."[5] When we "overfunction" like that, we typically make the other people (and ourselves) angry, become anxious, *and lose a bit of our own sense of being an independent self.* Ah, *there* is the mischief! When divorcing people find it difficult to unhook themselves from a lingering sense of responsibility for an ex-spouse, it may very well be because the marriage they are trying to end was riddled with overfunctioning. If in a marriage we have veered over into this danger zone, then we are going to find it all the more difficult to reclaim our "selves" in divorce. The rule of thumb I have learned to use after working with lots of divorcing people is simply this: the more a person has overfunctioned in the space of his or her ex-spouse, the harder it is going to be to detach from that partner and regain a sense of independent selfhood. Not impossible, mind you, just more difficult, and the primary way to overcome the difficulty is to come to a specific awareness of just how it is we have tried—and of necessity failed—to take the other's responsibility. That is the reason for writing about it here: not to saddle you with an impossible burden but to suggest a way to put it down, by examining in careful detail how you may have fallen into that trap, how you may have confused "bearing each other's burdens" with overfunctioning in each other's space.

Sometimes the overfunctioning goes on through a dynamic referred to in therapeutic circles as "triangulation,"

[5] Edwin H. Friedman, *Generation to Generation: Family Process in Church and Synagogue* (New York: The Guilford Press, 1985) pp. 210–12.

an insidious interpersonal arrangement in which we can easily get caught up without our wanting to or even knowing about it. The basic idea behind triangulation is that when two separate people experience difficulty getting together about something, they will tend to recruit a third party, who essentially has nothing to do with what is going on, to join the cause and make the connection the two original actors could not. That third party has then been "triangulated," which is to say, given the job of carrying something—an aspect of a relationship, an issue, a piece of behavior, a feeling, and so on—with which it originally had nothing to do. If the triangulation is "successful," then it comes to look as though the issue is between the third party and one of the two originals, letting the other original off the hook. Of course, because the third party is not inherently involved in what is *really* going on between numbers one and two, a great deal of disruption, pain, mystification, and issue-avoiding may (probably will!) take place. I have taken some care to speak of people *or* issues, because triangulation need not involve three human beings; it may just as well be among two people and one issue or experience or any other combination. Here are three examples to illustrate.

Melanie is a generally angry woman who flies off the handle easily, overreacts to situations, and often cannot find anything in reality to justify the level of anger she feels. She describes her father as a terribly difficult man to live with but her mother as a patient soul who never got angry at much of anything, least of all Melanie's father. Her approach to Melanie is typically symbolized by the recurring plea, "Now don't upset your father." In time Melanie comes to realize that she has been "triangulated" over the years: her mother was unable or unwilling to deal with her own anger toward her husband, and so Melanie as a little girl was given the "script" of being an angry, rebellious child and later adult, *particularly at her father.* As long as Melanie is acting out her mother's anger, Mother does not have to face and deal with it herself. That is the triangle: Mother, her anger, and Melanie.

Susan and Mark were a married couple with only one area of conflict, though it was severe: they typically spent holidays with Susan's parents, and every time that happened there would be a furious fight of some sort between Susan and Mark, invariably with the theme that Mark felt left out and ignored by both his in-laws and his wife, partly because of the way they treated him at these family get-togethers and partly because they never came to *his* (and Susan's) home to celebrate. In time it came out that Susan had been seriously ignored by her family both while growing up and later, including such things as her mother's nearly dying of a life-threatening illness and Susan's never being told of it, though she was an adult at the time. She was inwardly furiously angry at her parents for excluding her so, but since she was unable to deal with them about that, she and they had unconsciously conscripted Mark into the role of "excluded one" so that now he, rather than his wife, was the one carrying the problem and the feelings, while Susan and her parents seemed to be having pleasant, intimate family times. The triangle: Susan's feeling of exclusion, her parents, and Mark.

Geoffrey was seriously overinvolved in his wife Jennifer's performance problems as a schoolteacher. He chronically worried, got depressed, tried to help her with her work when she did not want it, and finally got very angry at Jennifer for lacking self-confidence and at her school for not being supportive enough of his wife. In reality Geoffrey had been triangulated into the otherwise straightforward relation between Jennifer and her work (although, of course, with his own unconscious acquiescence, having to do, no doubt, with unresolved triangles from his own family experience) so that he was doing the emotional "work" for her, allowing her to muddle along with mediocre performance but not a great deal of anxiety about it.

It needs to be said clearly that divorce is not in and of itself a cure for triangulation. On the contrary, a good deal of the trouble I see divorcing people in has to do with their *remaining* in a triangulated relationship with former spouses, children, or in-laws, even though a divorce may long since have occurred. What is necessary is a careful thinking through—perhaps with professional help—of the relational patterns one finds oneself in, so that other people's issues can, in effect, be handed back to them to deal with, rather than roping in another person through overfunctioning or triangulation. Only then, with part of the self thus returned to its owner, can we really talk about mutual responsibility and service, as we do in the next section of this chapter.

In saying all this I cannot emphasize too strongly that caring, intimacy, helpfulness, empathy, and personal support are *not* the same as "overfunctioning," doing other people's work for them, taking on their responsibilities, or being involved in a triangulated relationship. I take seriously that the source of a lot of overfunctioning is people's genuine desire, perhaps based on the spiritual values of sharing and helpfulness reflected in the wedding vows themselves, to share their mates' lives "for better or worse." That is why bearing each other's burdens so easily crosses the line from appropriate support and empathy to inappropriate taking over responsibility. It will not surprise you, from what I have written earlier about the Galatians text, that I am not too keen on that particular verse or idea as the basis for the kind of interrelatedness a relationship needs (except in its "narrow," biblical sense). If we wanted a better image to gather up our concern, I would suggest something like Paul's admonition in Romans 12:15: "Rejoice with those who rejoice, weep with those who weep." That whole chapter, in fact, is a remarkably astute theological statement of what it means to love and live with other people *without* violating their boundaries. Rejoicing with those who rejoice and weeping with those who weep is a posture and experience that puts me most intimately *with and for* a person without either *displacing* any part of what it is they themselves must live out or surrendering a part of myself in such a way that I no longer have it to use or give.

GOOD SERVANTS ARE HARD TO FIND

The third aspect of the return of the self I want to talk about has to do with that favorite old Sunday School idea of being a "servant." Those of us who were raised in the church cut our teeth on this one—and possibly chipped some into the bargain. Much of the whole Judaeo-Christian ethic is gathered up in the image of the servant—the person who serves others rather than getting served. The whole idea is that if everybody in the society embodies that ethic then in fact everyone *is* served, though not because we set out to get that for ourselves. In marriage, as in life in general, the value of setting one's own needs aside in order to serve another—say, one's partner—is what makes society work. In the New Testament Jesus makes it the primary ethical paradox: if one would be "greatest," then one takes the role of the least—the servant.

The possibility of distortion in that value is very much like what we have already been talking about: that an offering of the self in service gets confused with a *denial* of the self. When that happens we have to say pretty clearly and firmly that *serving and self-denial are not at all the same things.* When it comes to divorce, a person who is having heavy going with the separation may have fallen into that confusion. Time after time I hear divorcing people ask something to the effect of "What right do I have to seek my own happiness when I am supposed to be serving the needs of someone else?" meaning an ex-spouse or children or perhaps the marriage itself. Isn't it basically disloyal, divorcing people often ask? To answer that I want to suggest a slightly different way of thinking about the meaning of loyalty, and what it means to "work" in a relationship.

I no longer remember where I first heard the idea, but somewhere along the line in working with the personal dynamics of human organizations I came across the following conception of what "loyalty" meant in an organizational setting; I believe it works equally well to help us understand what loyalty means in the "organization" of marriage, and subsequently in divorce. What we think of as "loyalty" is really a composite of four separate loyalties, and they operate rather differently. Each loyalty represents a certain kind of inner *commitment*, expressed through certain *reliable behavior*, which means *allegiance* to some things but detachment from others.

First there is loyalty to a *person or persons* in the organization. Loyalty to them means I am committed to whatever part of their well-being is involved in the organization, acting that out through such behaviors as truth-telling, being available to them, seeking ways to help them, and so on. My allegiance to them means that some other people are further down the list of where my work and energy goes, to the point that some people may have to be taken off the list altogether. When the "organization" is a marriage, personal loyalty means such concrete things as being sexually faithful to a spouse, modifying or withdrawing from certain previous opposite-sex friendships, devoting myself to children, sometimes putting my family's needs and claims ahead of other people's, and all the many and varied things we usually think of as claiming our commitment in the personal dimension of marriage.

Second comes loyalty to the *ideal* or major purpose of the organization. To the extent I am loyal to an organization's ideal I "buy" it and believe in it as something worth committing myself to without cynicism or profiteering. In marriage this kind of loyalty spells the difference between believing in what the relationship ideally means and can be, on the one hand, and just going along for the ride or my own convenience on the other. Loyalties are never perfect, of course, and motivations for both getting and staying married always include some less than "ideal" ingredients. It is when the balance tips over toward the crassly pragmatic and convenient that we could appropriately speak of someone's having less than enough loyalty to the ideal or major purpose of marriage—however that is conceived by different people and in different cultures.

The third kind of loyalty has to do with the actual ongoing *work* of the organization, what happens day in and day out to keep it functioning, even when the connection between that work and the ideal may seem remote indeed. The point here is that regardless how I may feel about the person or the ideal, this kind of loyalty is expressed through carrying on what needs to be done in my role as marriage partner. This, in other words, is sometimes where the "for better or worse" clause of the marriage vow calls in its chips.

The fourth strand of loyalty is to the *institution* itself, a fine difference from the matters of either ideal or work. In organizational terms there is a dimension of my service to it that relates to the fact that this particular type of endeavor, this "institution," has a worth and claim on me because of the very kind of thing it is. For instance, I teach in a theological seminary composed of many different *people*, a set of *ideals* having to do with the training of ministers and service to the church, and a complex *work* involving teaching students and administering the school. But in addition to that there is *the institution itself,* occupying a place in history both as the particular seminary it is and as one of many such places that make up the still larger "institution" of theological education. That, too, lays claim to a strand of my inner commitment, behavior, and allegiance—my loyalty. The same is to be said of marriage as an "institution." A colleague once commented, for instance, that though marital therapists often believe a couple should divorce for the sake of the best interests of everyone involved, and though many marital therapists are themselves divorced, nearly all of us are "pro-marriage" in our basic orientation. What he was referring to by that was loyalty to the institution.

Now what does all this have to do with the divorcing person's experience, especially his or her worry about having failed as a loyal "servant" in a marriage? It has two things to do with it, basically. The first is to let us see that loyalty or service is a complex matter involving more different commitments, behaviors, and attachments than we might first have thought. Blanket, overall judgments about disloyalty must be looked at in finer detail both by divorcing people and those who surround them. The second thing this point of view does is to allow us to say that in divorce people have the opportunity not to lay down their loyalties so much as to *transfer* them to a new reality that also exerts its claim for service, the reality of the divorcing relationship. Let us see how that may operate with each of the kinds of loyalty or service.

In divorce my loyalty to the persons involved changes character and direction. Hopefully it will be as strong as ever as far as children are concerned. Toward a former spouse, however, the personal loyalty now has to do not with the love of a marriage partner, fidelity, or even for that matter basic liking, but rather with the responsibilities laid down by the divorce arrangements, including such things as respecting a former mate's personal boundaries, letting him or her live their own lives, not trying to get personal revenge through backbiting, sabotage, or using children as spies and mercenaries, and the like. Divorcing people are sometimes heard to say that no matter how much they despise their ex-mates, they nevertheless hold them in a certain positive light—perhaps involving respect or support—as the parents of their children. That would be an expression of a transferred personal loyalty in divorce.

Loyalty to the ideal of an ended marriage obviously changes rather radically because I no longer hold it as an ideal for myself. Even still, some surprising elements may remain in divorce. For instance, part of the marital ideal was providing a nurturing society for the raising of my children. Now my loyalty to that part of the ideal is transferred intact to the divorcing situation, the difference being that the former marriage is not itself a part of it. Or again, part of the marital ideal may have involved the personal and professional development of the partners, and my transferred loyalty in divorce may mean that I try to "conduct" the divorce so that my former mate's ongoing development is hindered as little as possible. Perhaps most basic of all, however, is being able to attach my ideal loyalty to a future relationship in which it may be able to live again. That, too, I would argue, is in a paradoxical way a transfer of one of the loyalties of a failed marriage in the divorcing situation. I have seen too many subsequent marriages in trouble because either or both of the new partners had been unable to transfer their loyalties from the ideal of a previous marriage to the current one.

The work of the failed marriage is now over, but it has been replaced (as these pages have been trying to show) by the work of the new divorcing relationship—very different in kind but in its own way equally demanding of loyalty and service. I often find myself wishing that people could give themselves due credit for making a divorce work well. Everyone applauds for people working well at a marriage; why not the same for divorce? More to the point, since trying to change social attitudes and biases is an ongoing form of windmill-jousting, what I want to do is encourage divorcing persons to give *themselves* credit where it is due, and to commit themselves to managing the kind of divorce with freedom that merits it. That, too, is loyalty.

Finally, even though people often emerge from failed marriages looking like the walking wounded, there is ample evidence that the majority of them are eventually game to try it again. Whether they realize it or not they have transferred, not lost, their loyalty to the institution of marriage. To be sure, there may be—some would say there even *should* be—an interim period during the grieving of divorce in which remarriage is unthinkable, so badly shaken has been one's loyalty to the institution. That can also be, however, a "seeds within the snow" period, as Krantzler says, during which one's view of marriage changes, perhaps matures, comes into closer alignment with what one realistically can aim for and genuinely wants.[6] It is not Pollyannaism to say that a divorce can teach you something important and positive about what marriage is, ought to, and might yet be.

Good servants are indeed hard to find, as the old cartoon image suggests. What I have been trying to show in this section is that divorce does not *have* to mean one has struck out in the loyal service department (no matter how badly one may have bungled a marriage). Divorce can, by contrast, be an opportunity to transfer service and loyalty to something else, which amidst great pain and confusion has become a part of our new reality. When that happens the spiritual journey of divorce goes on.

[6] Mel Krantzler, *Creative Divorce: A New Opportunity for Personal Growth* (New York: New American Library, 1973) pp. 45 ff.

ELEVEN

Bridges over Troubled Waters:
Understanding New Relationships

THE HEART of this chapter is a subject about which very little is really known in any systematic way but which virtually everyone in divorce has experienced: the special and often troubling dynamics of a new love relationship in the process. I have come to believe, partly as a result of my clinical work with divorcing people and partly from my own experience of divorce and its aftermath, that a certain kind of relationship often occurs and is in fact needed as part of the divorcing process and journey, a relationship with its own intensity and meaning but one which in all likelihood is *not* a good candidate for permanency and remarriage. Though I may very well have left some stone I do not know about unturned (and would be very glad to hear of it), my research does not find any treatment in the vast literature on divorce and remarriage of this particular bond, which I will now be calling, in the terms of a well-defined psychological school of thought, "the transitional relationship."

Let me begin with a plain English description of what I mean and the theory I have about it. The evidence is strong that most divorcing people get involved in a romantic relationship with a new partner somewhere along the line, sometimes before a marriage is over (and often as the "reason" for ending it) and sometimes long after, *which, however, does not last long enough or proceed harmoniously enough to lead to a stable remarriage.* It is different from other new liaisons. As I say, we have long noticed that that is true for large numbers of people. Usually, however, observers and writers have more or less shrugged it off as some kind of "practice round" phenomenon and not asked very much more about it. After all, we reason, fairly few pairings are of the storied love-at-first-sight variety; most of us date several people before finding the one we want to enter a permanent relationship with, and there is no apparent reason things should be so different in renewed courtship following a divorce.

Sensible a position though that is, however, it overlooks something many divorcing people can quickly tell you: *something* about one or more of those relationships often feels very different from the others we experience and know about. There is something more intense about it, perhaps more reckless; it may feel like the sort of thing you thought you were too old for, the "falling in love again" you could have sworn had passed you by. Sometimes spiritually oriented people will have a feeling of the relationship's being somehow preordained, written in the stars, or bestowed by God. Still, in the end this particular relationship goes away, either dramatically or quietly, and we move on. This is the "transitional relationship"—common, important, but poorly understood.

We know very well, for instance, that a good many adulterous affairs that occasion divorce are really an unconscious way for a partner to end a marriage he or she is dissatisfied with but unable to confront directly. In those cases it is not so much a matter of a person leaving a marriage *because* he or she has found someone else as it is, in psychological fact, a matter of finding someone else as a way of leaving an unsatisfactory marriage. We know that a high percentage of those "exit affairs" do not come to any permanency. Sometimes a remarriage happens, all right, only to dissolve in a much shorter time than it took the first one to, but I believe more typically such relationships simply end. In other situations, where divorce has occurred without the presence of any third party, a person will strike up a relationship with a new partner that, no matter how intense or promising it seems to be, gets "stuck" and ends. Divorcing people typically report that they have been involved in one or more of these "steady" relationships before they find the person they ultimately remarry, if they do. Whatever the case, we have tended to mark these experiences up to the actuarial facts of life of divorce, so to speak, without asking whether there was some definable and important *work* being done by such relationships, something that those of us who are divorcing really ought to know about as part of understanding the whole process as a journey of the spirit.

Here, too, is where the value-laden question of loyalties and commitments enters the picture, often with a vengeance. What does it mean to a divorcing person to have another go at commitment when one has already failed? And what does it mean and say to us when that new attempt also "fails"? I have seen far too many people utterly demoralized and despondent about their own capacities for commitment because a transitional relationship has failed and they do not understand either why it did (and perhaps *had* to) or what it has done for them in the process. My basic position here, however, is that the very nature of a transitional relationship has to do with a person's learning how to enter into and eventually sustain new commitments to partners in love, and perhaps in new marriage. If the transitional relationship goes well and we can learn from it, then *whether or not it culminates in marriage,* it has played its own major role in the spiritual journey of divorce.

The concept of a "transitional" something-or-other comes from some pioneering work in psychiatry by the British child psychoanalyst D. W. Winnicott.[1] Chances are good you have not heard of him, but equally good you have not only heard of but experienced firsthand his major contribution to what we know about human development. Winnicott observed over and over again in his work with infants and children that they would choose certain "objects" as special favorites and invest them with extraordinary significance. We might be talking about a thumb (in the mouth) or a scruffy teddy bear or a well-worn baby blanket, or virtually anything else, as constant companions. These were the "security blankets" made famous by the character of Linus in Schultz's comic strip "Peanuts," and while they *are* undeniably comic at times, they are also psychological business of the first order for any and all children—and later, adults.

Winnicott and his later associates and followers developed a theory and an understanding of the significance of

[1] D. W. Winnicott, *Through Paediatrics to Psycho-Analysis* (New York, Basic Books, Inc., 1975). Winnicott's original article, "Transitional Objects and Phenomena," which is contained in this collection of essays (pp. 229–42), was first published in 1951.

these specially chosen things, which he came to call "transitional objects."[2] To the child they were a way of linking the two worlds in which he or she constantly lived: the inner, "all me" world of fantasy and magic, and the slowly emerging outer world of real objects, people, and events that the child, of necessity, was having to admit existed "out there," despite the inherent threat it posed to the safety of mother's breast. The transitional object served as a bridge between the two. It was, after all, a real thing that the child could identify and know about, as part of his or her body, or as a toy, or as a blanket. It was an "object" that was "not me" and had to be dealt with as part of that outer world. But at the same time, in the child's internal experience it was magically something else, an extension of himself/herself, a source of comfort and reassurance *over against* the rough-and-tumble of the outer world, which was very different from either the completely enclosed haven of the womb or the still relatively "all for me" security of the mother's breast. Transitional objects are one way a child deals with the fear and anxiety that come from the experience of moving out of a safe haven into the uncharted waters of the frightening real world. This emotional significance explains the experience every parent has had who has made the fatal error of trying to remove, wash, or in any other way improve the transitional object. Howls of protest and deprivation were probably the result, and only the most savvy of parents tumbled to the fact that it was a virtual extension, in a magical way, of the child himself/herself we were trying to pry the child away from. The wisest of us gave up and held our noses. In time children relinquish their transitional objects, without fanfare or mourning, with in fact little to mark the profound significance they had for the perilous

[2] Simon A. Grolnick and Leonard Barkin, eds., *Between Reality and Fantasy: Transitional Objects and Phenomena* (New York: Jason Aronson, 1978).

journey of those early years. The Velveteen Rabbit simply goes to the attic.[3]

Gradually a whole theory of human development emerged from Winnicott's basic observation. He believed, for instance, that one important residue of early transitional experience was to be found in creativity, "in the intense experiencing that belongs to the arts and to religion and to imaginative living, and to creative scientific work."[4] Beyond that, however, the theory holds that whenever human beings are confronted with the need for radical adaptation to a changed outer world, they do so by using the adult equivalents of their childhood security blankets, by relying *in a temporary and entirely appropriate way* on transitional objects and phenomena—which can be as diverse as therapy or a therapist or a favorite possession or a habit like knocking wood or smoking a cigarette—as a bridge between the protected inner world of fantasy and security and the threatening outer world of new demands and experience. There is nothing wrong with that; it is the appropriate use of a bridge over troubled waters, and like the child's transitional object that in time is abandoned, so, too, these adult transitional experiences do their work and are then restored to "real world" status.

One of the least investigated aspects of the whole transitional phenomenon is the question of how *people and relationships* sometimes function as transitional experiences in exactly the same way. No one in this school of thought doubts that they *do*, but at the same time the *way* they do is murky. And yet I believe that in the divorcing person's experience of new relationships the transitional phenomenon is crucial—and common if not universal. What I am suggesting, in other words, is that some early significant

---

[3] Children's literature is full of stories involving transitional objects, one of the most classic of which is Margery Williams' *The Velveteen Rabbit: Or How Toys Become Real*, now available in several editions from several publishers.

[4] Winnicott, p. 242.

relationship in the divorcing process is probably a "transitional" one whose deep emotional purpose is to help the divorcing person learn to live and love in the real world of the formerly married. Like all transitional phenomena, when this kind of relationship has done its "bridging" work, it becomes something very different from what it was. The magic is no longer in it, nor is the incredibly strong attachment of its owner. In all likelihood it will be set aside, or at least put in its proper place in the lineup of real world objects and relationships. The favorite teddy eventually goes to the attic with the child's other toys; the security blanket is finally washed and put away (though perhaps it will still be useful for warmth from time to time), and so, too, the transitional relationship either ends or radically changes—back into a friendship, perhaps, instead of a romantic bond.

Again and again I have worked with new couples, one or both of whom are in the divorcing process, who have found each other almost as the answer to prayer. No therapist likes to rain on people's parades, but painful though it is, it is necessary for me to gently get the message across that what this wonderful relationship may be doing is not leading to permanency, as the couple believes and hopes, but rather helping them to move ahead in the divorcing process. I will sometimes say, bluntly but I hope charitably, that *if* the relationship is going to be permanent, it is going to have to "end" first (as a transitional relationship) and perhaps then be reconstituted as a more enduring, real-world one. (I am often not very sanguine about the chances for that, but in theory at least it can happen.) George and Esther, for instance, were about as demonstrably devoted a couple as I have seen. There is something simply touching about people in their fifties holding hands and finding each other "cute." These two were both going through highly conflicted and painful divorces, hotly contested by the respective spouses and their nearly adult children. They had met in the midst of all the furor when George, who was a minister, had a brief pastoral encounter with Esther, a visitor to his church. Lights flashed, bells went off, and they found in each other not only wonderful romantic excitement but equally a deep sense of mutual healing and support. They planned to be married as soon as their divorces were final. In the process George was called to be pastor of another church, and they planned the move together, taking responsible care for the proprieties of the situation but being quite open with people about their "engaged" status. In counseling we worked on a number of important things, including their rages at their soon-to-be former spouses, their guilt at leaving marriages of over twenty-five years' duration, and their fearfulness about starting over again. Early on I had told them my belief about the transitional relationship, and urged them to be on the lookout for—and not be panicked by—signs that what they meant to and gave each other were changing. *An important part of that message was to affirm that transitional relationships are real, important, and to be valued even if they must come to an end short of the place the new partners have in mind.*

Predictably, George and Esther believed not a word of it. And just as predictably, in time the magic began to recede. They would and should mourn *this* loss just as they did their marriages. My hope, though, was that they would not see it as a "failure" or an exercise in despair, because in the light of what a transitional relationship is supposed to do it had not failed at all: it had allowed them to bridge that yawning gap between being married and single, so that each was now ready for something very different—not impossibly to each other, but perhaps not very likely either.

When we ask what a transitional experience does, psychologically speaking, we come to largely uninvestigated territory. Taking a clue from what is more generally

known about transitional objects and phenomena, however, and looking as closely as I can at the clinical experience of myself and others, I would suggest at least three
things.

*First, the transitional relationship restores confidence in the
self.* In the previous chapter we talked about the recovery
of the self in divorce, and it seems to me that the transitional relationship can be a vital ingredient in the way
that happens. That is precisely what is going on with the
child's security blanket. The child is learning what it is
like to be an entity in a world of *other* entities. The boundaries around the child's experience, which give the child a
sense of being a durable and identifiable "self," get built as
he or she crosses back and forth over a transitional-object
bridge between "all me" magic and "not me" reality. One
of the things divorcing people know full well is that their
own senses of "self" can get badly shaken in the process.
This "me" I had thought of as a person capable of love,
loyalty, commitment, humor, and family responsibility
turns out to be consumed by anxiety and loneliness, full of
anger, detached from the spouse its world had once re-
volved around, sour and humorless much of the time, and
removed either wholly or in part from its once dominant
family. Is it really "me" at all? One way I have of finding
out is by taking the chance of getting close to another
person, but in such a way that it is not quite "real"—or to
be more accurate, in a way that is more real than real. The
transitional relationship is born.

There are obviously many ingredients involved when
we speak of restoring confidence in the self in this way,
but two in particular stand out as frequently dominant in
the divorce experience. One is a person's sense of sexual
competence and the other is one's sense of the possibility
of making significant attachments to others. It is common
for both those things to be badly shaken by divorce.

In my clinical experience I have rarely encountered a

troubled couple, especially one headed for divorce, whose sexual life remained free from deterioration. Along with decreased sexual performance and satisfaction tends to come a feeling that one is just not *able* to do what conceivably was once both easy and a source of justifiable self-satisfaction. Sometimes the feeling that one is an inadequate lover is an extension of the similar feeling (and perhaps plain fact) that one has not measured up as a wife or husband, at least in this relationship. A good sexual experience in a transitional relationship often brings fresh perspective and confidence into the picture, sometimes to the relieved amazement of the divorcing person, who discovers that he or she is a good lover, after all, once out of the toxic atmosphere of a dissolving marriage.

I want to make as sharp a distinction as I can between this regaining of sexual confidence and promiscuous libertinism. The common enough phenomenon of divorcing people bed-hopping with abandon right after separation or divorce seems to have more to do with acting out grief and anger than with regaining sexual confidence (though admittedly in practice they may be hard to separate). One night stands are *not* what I mean by transitional relationships.

Closely related to sexual self-confidence is one's belief in his or her capacity for attachment to another. I choose the word "attachment" with some care, rather than "commitment," which is sometimes used as a synonym. Here it is not. The first question after divorce is not so much whether I can sustain a "commitment" to someone else over time, but rather more basically whether I can attach myself *at all* to someone in an intimate, caring way. Do I still have the capacity to know what it feels like to be in love, for instance? Can I experience the normal reversals and disappointments of any relationship in a way that does not send me running to the lifeboats for fear the whole ship is sinking? Can I let my guard down enough to let someone get close to me, physically, emotionally, and even spiritually? These are the kinds of questions the transitional relationship helps us answer. The very unreal, "magical" quality of it is what lets me take the sometimes enormously high risk of asking them in the context of an actual (rather than imagined) attachment.

Second, the transitional relationship serves as emotional protection against the deep, primitive, childlike fear of abandonment and annihilation that often happens in divorce. It may not be a very conscious experience at all, by the way. As adults we tend to forget that for the small child the fear of its parents' abandoning it is tantamount to the fear of literal annihilation. Something of that same drastic significance continues to cling to abandonment fear and experience even after we are grown up and "know" that literal, physical survival is not really at risk. Divorce, even when we may be the ones who did the actual leaving, brings that fear to the surface. Curiously, for instance, both my ex-wife and I, while being inherently private people with both a tolerance and a need for considerable solitude, chose living arrangements right after our separation that put us in constant and unaccustomed contact with other people: I by moving to an apartment complex (which I had sworn I would never again live in!) and she by taking in a neighbor to live for a long period while the neighbor's house was being renovated. Both those moves were somewhat out of character, and are a bit of evidence, I believe, for the presence of the kind of fear I am now talking about, even in two people who by outside observation might have been thought relatively immune from it.

In another example, I vividly remember becoming conscious of the fear in myself the first time I was ill after divorce. I had to have some uncomplicated local tennis-elbow surgery, and was well surrounded by friends. But for a little while beforehand the utter aloneness of the experience was nearly overwhelming, something very like what a child experiences when the child fears his or her parents are not going to return.

My own experience with transitional relationship was particularly vivid in this respect and may not be all that different from many others'. I learned in the process that, given my own psychological history and makeup, I was especially vulnerable to fears of rejection and abandonment, a theme that divorce only made more pronounced. With unerring psychic accuracy I unconsciously "chose" transitional partners who would in fact do just that to me, leaving me either physically or emotionally out in the cold from time to time. In the process I "learned" at least three things: first, that painful though it was, I could indeed survive that abandonment and therefore was protected from the deepest fear of it; second, that as a result I could risk fully involving myself in a relationship rather than holding part of myself back against the day it might be over; and third, that having had this sort of transitional experience, I no longer needed, consciously or unconsciously, to choose a partner who was going to be in some way unavailable. The positive outcome was a paradox: because I had been helped with my childlike fear of abandonment, I no longer needed to keep acting it out by getting involved with people who were going to trigger it; and hence I was no longer afraid of being involved with someone who was for sure going to stay put with me.

Third, it seems clear that the transitional relationship can help the grieving process, particularly when the new relationship itself ends. I have already talked about how divorcing people sometimes do not consciously feel that they are grieving, especially when the separation is something they themselves actively wanted. Sometimes that grief is experienced almost vicariously in and through transitional relationships. I have seen it work in three dominant ways. In the first one a person finds qualities and behaviors in the transitional person that remind them of their former spouse, either negatively or positively, and that, in turn, elicit feelings of loss that could not be experienced from thinking *directly* of the ended marriage. Ellen, for instance, burst into tears the first time her new friend Steve met and played with her young children. Her ex-husband had seldom had either time or motivation to do so, but she herself had been so busy "coping" with the divorce she had not been able to experience the grief over what her husband and her marriage had missed out on in this re-spect. Her tears at seeing Steve happily playing with the children their father had neglected were in fact tears over the marriage and both its lost opportunities and qualities it had never had. A positive version of the same experience would be when a person finds his or her new transitional friend embodying characteristics that had been welcome and loved in the ex-spouse, and grieves because they are now gone.

A second way the grieving process is helped becomes apparent when the transitional relationship hits a rough spot or even ends. I described in Chapter Eight my own experience of displaced grief, in which the strength of my feelings over the departure of a new friend actually repre-sented unexpressed feelings about the ending of my mar-riage. That new friendship was just such a transitional relationship, and in its very ending it did me a great ser-vice by unstiffening my upper lip and letting me get on with the grieving process.

There is little doubt in my mind now that I was work-ing through a lot of otherwise unexpressed feeling about my marital ending in and through the ending of the tran-sitional relationship. Here was a more direct and visible way of getting at some of the basic behaviors and feelings of ending a marriage that at the time were clouded by the other complicating issues associated with divorce—finan-cial arrangements, children, creating a new home, and the whole array of individual conflicts and emotional interchanges that make divorce such a complex psychological battleground. The feelings I had about not being married to my wife of many years were in some ways buried under the business of starting life on my own. The various facets of our conflictedness drew my attention away from the bedrock emotions of loss. In a transitional relationship, however, without those other arrangements and issues to contend with, the bare bones of the alliance, so to speak, were clearer: knowing what it felt like to trust a person and perhaps have it come to naught; realizing how much I depended on another person; acknowledging how much of my attachment involved the need to change and "rescue" the other person; discovering what qualities I most wanted—and most dreaded—in a partner; owning what I felt about my own sexuality and the risky business of offering it in vulnerability to another. All those issues— in whatever version of them applies to your own situation —are there in a marriage and its ending, but they can be devilishly hard to get hold of in the blizzard of *other* things one has to think about in divorce. In a transitional relationship they are often more visible; and when it ends, one comes to realize just how important they had been all along in his or her marital ending, though perhaps unseen or unacknowledged. Now they can and must be met head on, and it is not at all unusual to find that one's feelings about ending a new relationship are a reenactment, at a new level of consciousness, of what one had failed to do in the old. Perhaps so far as grieving goes, then, we can make a better job of ending a transitional relationship than we did at ending a marriage, and so achieve a sense of emotional closure that would otherwise be lacking.

A third way transitional experience helps the grieving process applies to that group of divorcing people (such as myself) who are in mid-life, and perhaps especially who are male. (What follows may very well apply, with some modification, to women as well, but unfortunately the main studies of adult development have been with male populations.) Because mid-life divorce is not only common (some would say increasingly so) but much in the public eye, let me make this particular point at somewhat greater length than the previous two about the connection of transitional experience to grieving.

One of the essential tasks of the mid-life transition is grieving for the various dreams, capacities, and opportunities that we had when younger but that now are beyond us or nearly so. That, too, is a loss experience of epic proportions, as I take stock of all the things I will never be able to do either because time or opportunity has run out or because my changing ("aging," I am forced to admit, is the correct term!) physical-emotional-spiritual person will not allow them anymore. Even such admittedly silly things as fantasies about being elected President of the United States or becoming a championship figure skater or concert musician have to go. Mid-life people sometimes go to heroic lengths to stave off that necessary developmental grieving; that is one of the main things the so-called "mid-life crisis" is all about.

What all this has to do with transitional relationships is simply that such a relationship may for a time try to turn back the developmental clock but in its ending bring us back to the reality of who we are in the here and now. That seems to me particularly true for mid-life men who following divorce (or, as I have said before, as a seeming "cause" of it) get involved with much younger women. The rather cynical popular interpretation of such behavior (which seems quite frequent, though I have seen no good statistics on it) believes that the men are trying to stay young by choosing younger partners. Cynicism aside, there is a strong sense in which that is plainly true, as we try to avoid the mid-life grief over diminishing life returns by unconsciously casting ourselves in the roles of younger men—often right down to fantasies (and often, of course, the actual thing) of having children again and starting a new family.

From the perspective of a spiritual journey, however, one need not be so cynical. One can rather acknowledge that something like that is indeed going on, and that the transitional quality of the relationship is a way to confront and ultimately resolve it. Painful though it is, when I grieve over the loss of a transitional partner who was half a generation or more younger than I, I may also success-fully get on with the business of mid-life grieving for the young man I no longer am and the things he will no longer have a chance to do.

As I write this I am acutely aware of a dimension of it that may at first seem a bit callous or even crass, almost as though the "other" in a transitional relationship were be-ing used for our own purposes rather than related to as a human being with his or her own wants, needs, and integ-rity. Please be assured that I intend nothing of the kind. The transitional relationship is above all *real*, carrying with it all the responsibilities and opportunities of any human relationship, especially one based on love.

It is undeniably painful when one person in such a rela-tionship is having a transitional experience while the other is not, when in other words the other person wants and is ready for a more enduring, "real-world" relation-ship than is likely to happen, given the circumstances and the cast of characters. I am not naive enough to suggest, even if it were possible, that the divorcing person should announce at the outset that what is about to happen is a transitional relationship, thank you, and may not there-fore turn out quite the way we would like. Most of what we experience in such ways is, I suspect, unconscious and "over-the-shoulder," known only after the fact in retro-spect. "So that's the way it was," I may say to myself with an odd mixture of relief, insight, and sadness. It does not mean we set out to "use" a person or a relationship as just another stepping-stone on the divorcing trail. I have never encountered anyone who did that and I want to be very clear I am not recommending it. In fact, I rather doubt it is possible, given the complicated way human feelings unfold, any more than it is possible for a child to go shopping for what it already knows is going to be its transitional object. They *happen*, and later we may understand what it was that happened and why.

What I have tried to do in this chapter is probe and describe some of the inner dynamics of such a relationship, and in the process it may very well sound either utilitarian or manipulative. That, I am afraid, is just a by-product of having to talk in this way about something as complex, emotionally involving, and perhaps beautiful as a human relationship. Even on a spiritual journey, after all, one has to watch where the feet are going and pay some attention to rocks in the road and low-hanging branches overhead. That is by no means *all* the journey is about, but it might be a pretty bruising experience if such details were not paid attention to.

I look back on my own transitional experience with a mixture of gratitude and sadness. The people who helped me are very real and very present to me, though in different ways now than then. "It just didn't work," we may be tempted to say in the green-room atmosphere of a drama just concluded. But the whole point is that in many ways the relationships *did* work, transitionally, even though that was a different outcome from what we may have hoped when it began. For that there can be all the regret and sadness of something that ended differently than we had intended when we set out, but there is also gratitude for the gift of learning and growing that the experience gave us on our unfolding journey.

TWELVE

The Misunderstood Help of Marriage Counseling

ENDING A BOOK about divorce with a chapter on marriage counseling may sound a bit like closing the barn door after the horses are out. My aim here, though, is to try to clear up some of the misconceptions about such counseling that seem especially troublesome to people involved with divorce—either as divorcing persons or as family, friends, or helpers of those who are divorcing. Again and again I encounter several popular myths about marriage counseling, each of which is destructive and misleading in its own way. It is time to put paid to some of those wrongheaded notions, by way of a brief epilogue on what marriage counseling does and does not do.

The first myth is the notion that the primary aim of marriage counseling is to save marriages. In point of fact, it is not, no matter how glad therapists (or ministers and others who serve in roles something like marital therapists) may be when marriages are in fact restored. Let me share the short description of marital therapy I usually give to couples just beginning treatment with me. I have an image for the marital therapy process that is unashamedly corny but essentially accurate. I came by it one day while watching my local volunteer fire department try to save a burning eighteenth century house in the village where I lived. Soon the fire was out, with part of the house burned and the rest suffering different degrees of smoke and water damage. Among the gathered onlookers speculation ran high about what the owner would do with the results.

It came to me then that I was watching—and smelling— an apt analogy to what I try to do with couples in marriage counseling. They come for help with any number of fires raging in the "house" of their relationship. Some are of long duration, involving communication and interactional patterns, while others may be such immediate crises as an extramarital affair or fighting that has gotten out of hand. *Whatever the case, my basic job as a therapist is to try to help them put out those fires, so that they, the owners, can then look at the result and decide what to do with it.*

The alternatives can then be seen and studied. Perhaps there has been no real damage and life can go on as before. Perhaps part of the house has been damaged and some renovation—major or minor—is called for. Or perhaps the damage has been so great that there is no real choice but to bulldoze with divorce and start over. Three operating principles are at work in such an approach, and people involved in marital therapy need to know them well.

(1) Little, if anything, can be done until the fires are put out, that is, until the sources of conflict and trouble are identified, understood, and to some degree ameliorated. *(2) Then it is the responsibility of the couple, working with their therapist, to decide what should now happen with the marriage,* the possibilities ranging, as I have said, from business as usual to divorce. *(3) The goal of the therapy and of my work as a therapist is not to "save the marriage" but rather to help these people reach a decision that best serves the interests of everyone involved,* including children, other family members, and perhaps even other parties not directly related.

The bottom line is that marriage counseling "succeeds" when all three things happen, *even if the decision taken is to end the marriage.* There are many marriages in which such destructiveness and compromising of personal potential is going on that to continue them would represent, in effect, a "failure" of the counseling process. Then too, of course, there are marriages that we therapists believe really could work but whose partners choose to end, to our sorrow. As I have said in previous pages, most marital therapists are pro-marriage; we would like nothing better than for the people in our offices to be able to make their relationships work well and reach the bright promises most, if not all, had or thought they had when they began. *But that does not mean our business is "saving marriages." Our job is helping people get into a position where they can decide for themselves what is best for everyone involved.*

A second myth is that somehow marriage counseling inflames the situation and increases the risk of (or actually causes) divorce. Everyone seems to know at least one couple who went for such help and wound up divorced, perhaps proclaiming loudly in the process that their so-and-so therapist really messed things up for them and counseling took them from a bad-but-livable to worse situation. Frankly, sometimes it happens. There are inept and even irresponsible therapists at work, just as there are ministers, lawyers, doctors, and every other profession. That, though, does not seem to be the main fuel of the myth.

What we need to keep in mind is that the way human nature operates, given the general culture's understanding of the therapeutic process, most marriages are already suffering considerable strain by the time they reach the counselor's office. Only a sadly small number of couples seek help early enough in the development of their difficulties that therapy could rightly be called a "preventive" approach. I believe I can say that in my experience every couple I have treated who eventually divorced had in fact already reached what I began this book by calling "first divorce" by the time they saw me, no matter how superficially harmonious things seemed to be. (By contrast, though I do not want to seem boastful, couples who have not already reached "first divorce" when they come for help typically fare well, get what relief they need for whatever brought them in the first place, and go on to improved and happier relationships.) In some cases I would have to say that, as best I could determine, the relationship was pretty well doomed from the start, owing perhaps to major characterological difficulties in one or both partners, or to such a poisonous mismatching of personalities that no one would have given them much of a chance. But in far more cases I find myself wishing they had come sooner because I am pretty well convinced that the fires could have been put out before so much of the place was consumed that demolition was the only alternative.

It is also undeniably true, by the way, that marriage counseling may be the occasion for heightened conflict and turmoil with a couple. Notice, however, that I did *not* say the counseling *caused* it, only that it was the *occasion* for it. There is a world of difference between the two. Leaving aside the comparatively rare case of gross mismanagement on the therapist's part, a large number of couples come for therapy precisely because they either do not know how to or are afraid to engage their issues on their own. They want and need the professional help of the therapist and the therapeutic milieu in order to take the lid off, so to speak, and what then emerges may be pretty inflammatory indeed. Naturally it is going to seem to an onlooker that the escalation of conflict coincided with doing the therapy. Indeed it did; it is just that the *causal* connection is not always there. What I have learned with such couples, moreover, is that *the degree of conflict or arousal* (perhaps we should speak more plainly of heat and decibel levels!) *almost never predicts the eventual outcome.* It is far more a question of how a couple handles their conflicts, what sort of resolution they are able to achieve, and what amount of irreparable damage has been done in the meantime that tells the tale of success or failure in the marriage.

A third myth is that marital therapy is limited to (or that getting it is an indication of) failing marriages. There are two somewhat more specialized forms of "marriage counseling" that are unfortunately not as common as they really should be, and I want to describe them briefly in the hope that some readers will be able to take advantage of them, or perhaps refer their families and friends to such resources. The first picks up the preventive theme mentioned earlier, and is counseling undertaken *whenever a couple's life circumstances and stress put it at emotional risk.* Particularly if there has been a history of discontent in the marriage, such things as retirement, geographical relocation, the birth or death of a child, the onset of chronic or terminal illness, economic collapse, unemployment, or disruption elsewhere in the couple's family system are all good and valid reasons for seeking professional consultation. The reason for that is simply that we know very good and well that such stressful experiences put people and marriages "at risk" of developing further difficulties.

Assessing just how great the risk is and what steps can be taken best to cope with it is the goal of such therapy, *whether or not overt marital conflict has appeared.* Tom and Martha were one such couple, in their late forties with college-age children when Tom was fired from his executive managerial position. Their styles of handling the unemployment and the various strains that put on family life were very different. Tom was relatively optimistic and somewhat carefree, while Martha was the eternal pessimist and increasingly resentful at having to work while Tom searched for a new job. Their therapy was a brief experience of several weeks exploring how they might handle those differences and helping them express and deal with the complicated feelings evoked partly by their crisis situation and partly by unresolved minor issues over the years. At the conclusion they had accomplished several things. They had taken stock of the nature of their situation rather than pulling the covers over their heads and hoping it would go away; they had discovered some coping resources they did not fully realize they had; they had worked productively on two or three areas of interpersonal conflict that in "normal" times were taken in stride but that loomed much larger in a crisis period; *and not to be overlooked, they had established a pattern of relating productively to a helping professional whom they could easily and comfortably use in the future whenever the going got rougher than they could handle on their own.* All of us in the practice of marital therapy wish we had far more Toms and Marthas on our doorsteps, so that the general level of marital discord and divorce might decrease across-the-board. I am being neither facetious nor evangelistic when I suggest that people need the familiarity of a therapist who knows them, just as they do a family doctor or dentist. A fair number of my counseling sessions are brief, special-focus interludes with people with whom I have previously worked in much longer term. They know when to come for help, and find that taking advantage of it shows the same good sense as getting anything repaired that they cannot easily do themselves. Coming back to their therapist is in no way a sign that somehow the earlier therapy did not work or was incomplete. Quite the contrary, it gave them a reusable resource for changing circumstances.

The second special form of marriage counseling is what is commonly called "divorce counseling," the work a couple does with a therapist either anticipating the possibility of a divorce or after the decision to divorce has been made. Contrary to much popular belief, the decision to divorce should seldom signal the end of marriage counseling but rather the beginning of "divorce counseling," with the same or another therapist, sometimes as a couple and sometimes individually.

Two foci are typical of divorce counseling, either before or after the actual decision. One is on the multitude of arrangements that have to be made in a divorce. The aim here is to help the divorcing spouses move toward the "divorce with freedom" pattern discussed in Chapter Two. It is naive to assume that deciding to divorce automatically means that detaching all the various connections of the relationship—both material and emotional—gets done without difficulty. The reverse is far more typically the case. Whether divorce can indeed become the sort of spiritual journey this book has been trying to describe may depend in large measure on whether good divorce counseling takes place.

The other focus of divorce counseling is perhaps more in keeping with what usually goes on in psychotherapy of any kind, namely helping the people understand the dynamics and patterns of what they are experiencing so they have at least a fighting chance of not getting caught in the same briar patch all over again. Granted, much of that kind of working-through can and should be done in individual therapy, but a great deal more than we often realize would really best be done by the divorcing couple together. I know that it goes against the grain of wanting to get things ended and over with (and perhaps wishing you never had to lay eyes on the ex-spouse again), but if some of that discomfort can be tolerated, the possibilities for a better divorce and future life are heightened considerably. As a therapist I wish more people could and would give themselves such an experience. It is one of the things that can spell the difference between divorce as a cataclysmic interruption of life and divorce as its own kind of journey with hope at the end.

Though I wish I did not have to, I nevertheless must address as a *fourth myth the still prevalent popular misconception that coming for marital therapy is a sign of weakness, something to be ashamed of, or maybe worse, the inevitable sign of a failing marriage.* I rather think the "shame factor" is an unavoidable consequence of our culture's pride in self-help and independence, as much as its fear of "craziness." What people do not always realize is that being a client or patient in any form of psychotherapy *is plain hard work* and the furthest thing from weakly or passively turning oneself over to an expert for fixing up.

As to therapy's seeming to be a concession of failure, people should realize that *any* marriage has its hairline cracks and hidden fissures, its potential conflicts and incompatibilities, which under the right amount of duress can widen and deepen to the point of putting the marriage in jeopardy. The question is not whether such fault lines are there, but rather whether the current context is stressful enough to make them dangerous. I believe most marital therapists would say that any marriage, no matter how smooth and ideal it is at the present moment, lives under the possibility of terminal crisis if the lethally "right" combination of contextual, intra- and interpersonal, social and historic forces comes into play. We are all potentially at risk, just as all of us harbor in our bodies a population of dangerous microbes that under the right circumstances can explode into illness or death.

The final myth is that marriage counseling is called for only when both spouses are unhappy and in conflict, and correspondingly that when only one of the two is having trouble with the marriage, the other one does not need help. That is a dangerously wrongheaded notion. Of course, there are lots of personal issues for which individual psychotherapy is needed; *but when the source of discontent even in only one partner has to do with the relationship itself, then it is the relationship that is the "patient" and has to be worked with.* A refusal of one spouse to come into marital therapy under such circumstances usually increases rather than decreases the chances of divorce as an outcome.

The reason for that is not hard to find. The spouse who comes alone for help is probably going to get it: he or she may become more insightful about the nature of the relationship, more confident in their own potential, freer in their acknowledgment and expression of difficult feelings, better able to take responsibility for their role in the marriage and its difficulties, and more ready to address conflict and not seek refuge in peace-keeping or denial. As that begins to happen, the spouse refusing to come into the process is going to be left further and further behind. What once was a relationship in equilibrium is quite likely to grow increasingly unbalanced as the growing spouse gains greater personal freedom and power, to the point that what was formerly endurable distress now becomes intolerable. The next step is divorce. The rule of thumb is that even if only one partner believes the relationship is in trouble, then in fact it *is* in trouble and in need at the very least of a thorough professional assessment with both partners. It is the relationship as a human system, not just the sum or combination of the two individual members, that is really the client in marital therapy. A stubborn, resistant, frightened, or arrogant spouse who refuses therapy is asking for trouble, and if divorce is the result, the spouse who came anyway for help need not feel the burden of responsibility for the breakup.

My aim here has been to give divorcing people and their associates a chance to do a little looking back over their shoulders at the therapeutic process (or lack of it) they may have experienced, so that they can understand a bit more clearly what they went through and why. Divorcing people often worry that their marriage counseling failed, that it made their marriage worse, that it was a sign of weakness, or that by coming for help alone they are responsible for the breakup. None of those things need necessarily be true, and if by discussing them in this way, we have lightened the load somewhat so that the journey is easier going, then my purpose will have been realized. If, by contrast, from reading this you realize that you made a mistake along the line, then my hope is that you will be better equipped in a future relationship. Some of the best motivation in the world for working well at another marriage is not wanting to have divorce happen again. Good luck and godspeed!

Epilogue

I BEGAN THIS BOOK with a personal word and want to end it the same way. In other books I have written I have said I thought the reader deserved to know something of what it was like for the author to "do this thing" and ask other people to join the process. This one is no exception.

If I have done my work with any basic skill, the pages you have read fit together more or less consistently, and my hope is that they have helped you look at the spiritual, valuational side of divorce in a different way than you might otherwise have. Possible appearances to the contrary, however, the result is by no means a seamless garment. I write this endnote nearly four years after the prologue, and I have tried to weave my own intervening experience into the text in such a way that it did not either intrude on what I was trying to say or interfere with the lives of people who were so intensely a part of it. The plain fact, though, is that the notion of divorce as spiritual journey is not something I have spied out from the sidelines so much as something I have picked and lived my way through during these years. They have been full of heartache, false starts, necessary though unwelcome learnings, exhilaration, promise, and what I can only describe as repentance. Thus it might be, I hope, with all of us. Now I both laugh and cry more easily, and I look out upon the future unfolding before me with both greater trepidation and greater hope than I ever did before. What makes it possible is that I realize more than ever something of what I have tried to speak about here, that I am both held and understood—by loving friends and grace-provided strangers, by children and family, by the woman I love with all my heart and have joined to continue this journey, and by the God who (if I may take a Calvinistic dare) is so much a part of my living and breathing I scarcely know how to describe it.

Thank you for sharing this odyssey. God bless you on your own.

Index

J. RANDALL NICHOLS is an ordained Presbyterian minister who has had extensive pastoral experience. He received his B.A. from Dartmouth College and his B.D. and Ph.D. from Princeton Theological Seminary. He is presently director of the Doctor of Ministry Program at Princeton Theological Seminary, as well as a lecturer in Theology and Communication there. He is also senior staff psychotherapist at Trinity Counseling Service in Princeton, New Jersey. He is the author of many publications, most recently the books *Building the Word: The Dynamics of Communication and Preaching* and *The Restoring Word: Preaching as Pastoral Communication.*